Hands Up?

Questions to ignite thinking in the classroom

Stephen Lockyer
With Jen Hart

This edition published by *Teacherly* in 2015.

Jennifer Hart is acknowledged as a contributor to this edition. Her insights into Secondary pedagogy and the structure were invaluable.

ISBN: 1505685621

Many thanks to all the teachers and friends who advised me along the way to writing this book, most especially Sue Cowley for her invaluable advice, as well as Jen Hart, David Rogers, Leah Sharp and Sway Grantham. I am also grateful to Toby French for his article and insight, as well as the support given to me by Peps McCrea and Martin Burrett. Thanks also to Emma Donovan for the brilliant original title name!

We have tried where possible to indicate the provenance of any ideas, but if you are able to help identify others for future editions, please do let us know. Thoughts/ ideas/ issues? Email **hi@teacherly.co** or find us on Twitter as @mrlockyer or @tchrly.

"If you can't explain it simply enough, you don't understand it well enough."

Albert Einstein

Contents

Hands Up: Questions to ignite thinking in the classroom

Introduction

You will find them in every school across the land, if you look carefully enough. In some schools they are common, a regular occurrence. In others you will need to look more carefully, search the classrooms, but they are there. In every school across the land you will find them, the **cloudholders**.

They are keen to contribute, eager to please and enthusiastic to the core. As you wander the halls you peer into classrooms and spot these mythical creatures. You look in with envy to a colleagues classroom and notice they have bred not one or two but a whole room full. You see the room is filled with hands up, urgently stretching for the heavens, each jostling to answer the question presented to them.

You wonder what spell has been woven to illicit such a response. What secret this teacher, this *magician*, holds that they have managed to cultivate these cloudholders, each desperate to contribute, eager to share their thoughts and ideas. You think back, despondent, to your own classroom experiences, and the contrast couldn't be vaster.

However, as with many stories, there is a twist in this tale. Cloudholders are not what, at first, they may seem. They are indiscriminate in their reach upwards. They cast a false impression for those that look upon their scene.

Look closer at that classroom, and you will see the image starts to unravel. *"Hands up if you want an early break?"* will generate an army of cloudholders in seconds. These duplicitous creatures fool the teacher they have successfully mastered the art of class discussion. The cruel irony being that the teacher themselves has created this species.

Is there anything more dangerous than the question asked which is so lacking challenge that everyone is able to answer, straight away? It's a fallacy that students like easy work, and their boredom threshold will quickly reveal how simple the teacher is making their work. Gradually, one by one, the cloudholders wither, they begin to cease thinking before responding and then eventually stop reaching at all.

Listen closer to the dialogue, which you longed to emulate and you will begin to see the cracks. You'll hear the teacher answering many of their own questions, dismissing the children's ability to contribute and letting exposition take precedence over learning. The false magician mistakenly believes that a complex answer requires a complex question, when in fact the reverse is true. The students find themselves spending more time unpicking the question than coming up with the answer.

Cloudholders are eager for recognition, for attention, but at any cost, without thought given to the quality of their answers.

Think again if you imagine a room of a cloudholders as a success story - as soon as you ask for hands up, you are subconsciously dividing the class up into those willing to share, and those that aren't. This book explores instead how to strip questions back to their fundamental purpose, how and why to repackage them, the many dangers and bad question practices which teachers of all service years can fall into, and the best techniques for making the most of questioning.

So, hands up if you want to improve?

How to get the most from this book

Like any learning process, you cannot expect to simply improve your questioning through simply reading these pages. Where possible, the theory, purpose and grounded reasoning behind different questioning strategies have been outlined in as much detail as is necessary. Almost all have practical tips and guidance, and are followed by a 'try this' section. It is strongly recommended you try only a few questioning strategies at a time. The accompanying workbook, "Hands Up Together" guides this slow growth. By dipping into this book according to need, you will supplement your ability to ask more insightful questions than you might at first expect.

Nomenclature:

The terms pupils, students and children are used throughout and are hoped to be interchangeable in the reader's mind.

Overview of Questioning

What is the point in questioning in the classroom? What are the key question types, and how do they operate? Underneath the bonnet of most questions is an underlying structure which is well-worth getting familiar with before exploring how you use questions in your classroom.

The Famous Five of Questioning

Who, what, why, where and when. These question leaders are our most common and a fine place to begin our journey into questioning.

In this section we will explore these different aspects of questioning and encourage you to reflect on your current practice. Through evaluating the way you utilise questions in your lessons you will then be able to explore how you can alter and improve the effectiveness of your questioning habits.

The average teacher will ask two questions per minute and up to 400 per day. With questioning making up such an integral part of our interactions with students, it is vital that we know why we are asking the questions we do and make them as effective as possible

Why are questions asked?

This is possibly the most important question to unravel. Without an understanding of why we ask questions then we are stumbling around without purpose. Imagine the classroom where all questions were removed; what would remain?

In this terrain there is an absence of dialogue, where teachers cannot clarify understanding of instructions, let alone depth of knowledge. Students cannot seek reassurance, guidance or explore their own intellectual curiosity.

This classroom is a staid environment where the absence of interaction is starkly felt and the teaching that remains is both didactic and ineffective.

There are a number of fundamental reasons why questions are asked in a classroom;
- Assessing the students current knowledge
- Logistical organisation
- Establishing progress within the lessons
- Clarifying instructions and details of tasks
- Encouraging and developing higher order thinking skills

For any one of these given purposes, different types of questions and techniques will be deployed subtly. There are many nuances of questioning which need careful consideration if you are not to waste the opportunity you have as teacher. It is perfectly possible to fill a lesson with questions, but not progress understanding, assess the students' learning or engage better, deeper thinking.

Try this

Make a prediction, are these five questioning purposes equally weighted in your lessons? Consider if they should be.

Ask a colleague to tally the types of questions you ask and compare the results to your prediction.

What is asked?

There are lots of different ways to classify questions and different questions will serve different purposes in the classroom. Whether you use Blooms taxonomy, DfES guidance or the latest university study, all classification systems will have a divide between lower and higher order question types.

Lower order questions are those which require factual recall and will generally be closed, with one correct answer and begin with; who, what, where or when. Higher order questions however will require a greater level of thinking on the students part. They are open questions where there are a range of answers and will subsequently require a deeper explanation by the students. Higher order questions tend to fall into the why, how or which categories.

It would be easy to jump on the bandwagon of assuming that all questions should be of higher order as these are the questions which promote the deeper understanding by the students. However, there are many reasons questions are asked in a classroom and low order questions do have important roles to play. For example it would be unnecessary to ask a probing question if your purpose is to establish that all the students in your charge have the ruler they will require for their graph work.

It has been demonstrated however that teachers ask far too many low order questions and insufficient higher order ones. This is possibly unsurprising, given, like the answers, these questions require less thought.

The ever so useful "*Why?*" is covered extensively elsewhere in this book, but if I were stranded on a Question Desert Island, this is the one I would save. It is the most powerful question in your armoury, both as a teacher and a learner, as it seeks consideration, depth and thought. Its cousin, *How*, runs a close second but works just as hard as a mental agitator. *Why* however is easier to use and understand. Details of how you can effectively deploy this grenade occur later in the book.

Try this:

Classify the questions below into High and Low order;

What is the capital of England?
What is the population of London?
What are the differences between London and York?
What reasons might people move to London?
What are the main causes of unemployment in a capital city?
What, in your opinion is the biggest draw for tourists to London?

You may have found some of these questions tricky to classify as the question itself could fall into either category dependent on the response elicited. For each of the above questions, consider how they could be amended in order to orchestrate a higher order response from the students.

Who is asking?

The default assumption when discussing questioning in class is to think about the teacher asking and the students responding. Indeed there is a whole chapter dedicated to improving the way in which you as a teacher plan and deliver your questions in class.

There are many questions asked within the classroom that may not be initiated by the teacher. I'd encourage you to consider your own classroom, do you have a monopoly on the questions?

The students themselves may ask questions out of necessity, to clarify instructions and seek reassurance from the teacher. They may also ask questions of each other, but is this actively encouraged in your classroom or is it managed as a low level disruption? Later in the book you will find a number of strategies to help encourage the students to contribute and to help manage these questions.

We should also not neglect the other adults who may venture into the classroom. Teaching Assistants, SEN support staff or technicians are all useful resources to be exploited.

The distribution of questions is also worthy of consideration, it is all too easy to be drawn in by the cloudholders. They are, after all eager to answer. Even when you are aware of those who are desperate to contribute you will fall into habits.

Try this

Ask the students to complete an exit ticket. Ask them to write down one question they have at the end of your lesson. Review the questions you have, what types of question are the students asking?

Where are questions asked?

Where we ask questions depends an awful lot on context, and this in turn leads to the type of questions we ask in those contexts.

It is important to reflect and identify the places you ask questions of your students, and more importantly, why you choose those places to ask those questions. It is easy (but naive) to assume that questions should largely remain in the classroom for example. If our children are to learn in an inquiry environment, it is wise to consider all the areas (in and out of school) we might be able to ask a probing, pertinent question of them, and see if we can't develop their thinking and learning as a result.

In the classroom

Questions in this environment need to relate to what the children have covered previously in class, what you are currently teaching them, and thinking about what the next stages are. No small feat! This seems like it would cover everything, but it is important to consider whether your questions are recounting and reflecting (past), developing and clarifying (the present), or predicting and summarisng (the future). Each of these three stages subtly suggests a different approach.

Consider:

What are the majority of your questions based in; the past, present or future of learning? How do you know?

In their books

While avoiding question widows, questions are an incredibly powerful way of taking learning and thinking on in a much more focused and intimate way than in a whole-class situation. By asking questions in a book, and encouraging a learning culture which requires a response, you are extending the children's thinking beyond simply "what mark did I get?" to one where they are reflective of their own learning and progress.

Consider

What was the last question you asked of a pupil in their book? Why did you ask it? Did they respond?

In their homework

Questions are powerful tools to use as a basis for homework. Designing a question which forces a reflective answer at the end of a topic can be one of the most effective ways of assessing their progress and understanding in your focus for the curriculum. Likewise, a series of closed questions can give you a quick tool for how strong their recall is of the topic (or how effective they are at searching on Google). Never waste a good half hour of homework with an inane question designed to fill time. This is a criminal waste of time.

Consider

Hands Up: Questions to ignite thinking in the classroom

Find the last item of homework phrased as a question. What did you hope the student would gain or demonstrate by answering that question?

In displays

Asking a question in a school display is covered extensively elsewhere in this book, but it is worth underlining that used judiciously, a good question can elevate a display from wall candy to learning buffet. Just as clever advertising can intrigue people enough to have them stop in their tracks, so too should a good display with an outstanding question.

Consider

Find the nearest display to you which has a question on it. What is the purpose of that question, and is there some way of answering it other than simply internally?

In revision

Revision questions are designed to take a litmus test of understanding for a forthcoming demonstration of the student's understanding. Simply rehashing previous questions may seem like common practice, but what is far more powerful is unpacking each of these questions with the students, and exploring each of the question's constituent parts. By doing this, you are making the question style more available and accessible to the pupils, not just the marking scheme for answers.

Consider

Find the last question you asked for revision. Why did you ask this? What was the response and what was your follow-up?

In Assembly

Don't ever underestimate the impact of a well-crafted question in an assembly. In one memorable Secondary assembly, we were asked, "if you didn't exist, would you be missed?" - a question which has both haunted and driven me ever since. These are questions which can be thoughtful morality seeds for the mind, of which call for gut responses from a large collective. Make them count.

When do you ask questions?

When you ask a question is dependent on many factors. In any lesson or topic, there are various moments when you can ask questions, and when certain questions are asked of you. How these are planned and distributed can have an impact on the benefit of that aspect of the lesson however, and this is very much teacher-led. Some teachers prefer no questions when explaining something explicitly to a class, while others appreciate questions at this point, since it can help to flesh out what you are speaking about, and it is attuned to the pupils' curiosities and interests.

Consider
When is the best time for questions from you? When is the best time for questions to you? How is this indicated in your learning environment? How might a new child identify this quickly?

Exploring your questioning patterns

Ask a colleague to identify the number of questions you ask, and the number of questions your students ask, over a set period of time (one lesson is ideal). Examine this information to see your patterns of questioning behaviour, what they reflect in terms of your teaching style, and where any significant gaps (that you perceive) may be. Break the rows below into times when the teaching format changes (for example, starter to exposition, to instruction, to directed work)

Hands Up: Questions to ignite thinking in the classroom

The Ten Commandments of teacher questioning

How do you ensure effective questioning? Good questioning takes time and effort to achieve, anyone who claims otherwise is either hopelessly naive or lying. With time and effort it can however become second nature, an automatic response to those eager faces before you.

Thou shalt track thy habits

Before beginning it is wise to establish what your biases are in class. Unless you are very aware, tacit habits can hide a multitude of sins in the classroom, and it takes one of two approaches to investigate this when examining your questioning skills.

The first thing needed is a simple sketch of your classroom layout, with the students clearly marked. If you can, indicate gender in some way, and mark out the class into four quadrants.

Next, carry out a 'typical' lesson, and either have a colleague observe you, or use the 'lesson study' technologies which are growing in popularity (see IRIS Connect for an example of these). During the lesson, mark down every time a child is chosen to answer a question. At the end of the lesson, examine this data on a range of variables - look at gender, popular or unpopular areas, even the abilities of the children. Does anything leap out as being imbalanced or skewed to one area/level? Look at ways to redress that balance. Why for example do you favour one side over the other - is it because of the design of your room? Children who miss out on being selected simply because of their seating position are being shortchanged in their lessons.

To take it further, although this would take a huge amount of time, carry out the same exercise and indicate how often each child indicates they have an answer, looking at the percentage they get asked, and a further percentage of how many times they are correct. This is the sort of information that becomes tacit over time with a teacher and class, yet can be misinterpreted easily, with biases hidden.

Although engagement is a word much-used yet hard to define (does passive engagement occur for example), the amount a student is *willing* to contribute to a lesson does have some reflection on their engagement with the learning. As personal proof, I only have to mention One Direction with some classes I teach to literally switch on the engagement of some children (and lose others).

You can always try a Learning Lent to mix your habits up. This is when you change something central to your teaching style - teaching from the other end of the classroom for example, or not using a computer when you would traditionally do so.

Try this
To demonstrate the effectiveness of this analysis, use a phone or tablet device at the back of your classroom and carry out the task yourself. You will miss key areas, but the gist will quickly become apparent.

Thou shalt stop answering thy own questions

Various estimates put the number of questions answered by teachers as between 50% and 80%! Imagine another environment where this was acceptable practice - how quickly would a confectioner go out of business if they ate 65% of their produce?

The desire to answer your own question is admittedly powerful, but the real puzzle is *why* we habitually do this. Sometimes this can be because we fear the silent pause and judge this to be a failed question. At other times, we worry that a delay in answering will damage the pace of the lesson (I'm certainly guilty of this). It may also be the case that the question being asked has been phrased in such a way that the students can't work out *how* to answer it.

Our train of thought can at times be so focused on the linearity of the lesson that answering questions is a natural extension of maintaining your internal dialogue. It is akin to a verbal tick and it feels entirely natural. Despite extensive self-reflection, I still answer my own questions a lot. I have however shared my need to stop this habit with my class, who fine me for every time it occurs.

Here is the solution then - stop it! Any question answered by you is a question unanswered by your students, and infers that you have a greater knowledge than their contributions (which in theory is correct, but isn't a message you necessarily want to encourage if they *are* contributing).

Instead, frame the answer you are seeking as a learning point or statement. It is a step, rather than a barrier, to their learning. Test this out - it's insanely hard to do, and requires constant reinforcement and practice.

Try this

Record the audio of your next teaching session, and tally how many questions you answer. Even conscious about this, you'll be surprised how often it takes place. Build in a reward/punishment for every time you are guilty of this - press-ups work well in my case.

Hands Up: Questions to ignite thinking in the classroom

Thou shalt use a 'no hands up' selection process

There is clear benefit in choosing a student to answer the question posed randomly. If we are to tackle those perpetual cloudholders we must make it the norm for students to be asked questions who haven't volunteered. By establishing a 'no- hands up' routine you encourage all to be ready with an answer.

Introducing this can initially encounter some resistance from the students. The most hardened cloudholders will continue to attempt to reach upwards, uncomfortable with a more level playing field. Their reach must be reduced but not acquitted; their enthusiasm should be maintained, while not indulging their need to be right.

It is worth investing the time in order to establish this routine as it will bring a myriad of benefits. If the students know that anyone of them could be asked to contribute, they must be prepared. They must remain attentive during the question posed and take time to formulate a response.

The old-fashioned method of 'choosing students at random' works perfectly well for a lot of the time. The tricky part is avoiding bias. As a teacher you must ensure that you are distributing your questions evenly and resisting the temptation to ask Elaine, the gifted child at the front, because you know she will be able to quickly provide an answer and the lesson will move on. Warning: this is really hard. Even when aware of this risk it is hard to avoid and there may well be other factors influencing your choice of *questestant.* An extreme example of this is a colleague of mine who realised she tended to neglect the front right hand section of the room. It took her no time at all to make the link between this was a blind spot in her vision, yet she hadn't realised it was happening until it was pointed out to her during an observation.

The greatest benefits of a random-name selector is that it can remove the inherent bias a teacher may have toward a particular group, gender or even area of the classroom, which of course naturally alienates one group while highlighting another. It offers one less thing to think about, and allows every child in the class (potentially) to be selected, with the aim that everyone is raising their game.

If you are becoming aware that you have biases at work, which is common (so don't feel guilty) or that you are missing key children out, there are methods for student selection that are worth exploring.

Lollipop sticks

This appeared to become fashionable overnight thanks to Dylan Wiliam demonstrating the technique to great effect on television. The idea is simple - each child in the class has a lollipop stick with their name on. A question is posed and in order to select a student to answer the teacher draws a lollipop stick from the pot.

Benefits
1. This is an excellent way to quickly become familiar with the names of the students in a new class.
2. As the question is posed before choosing the questestant , all students must ready themselves with a response.
3. Students can be allowed to decorate their own lollipop stick which can help get student 'buy in' quickly when introducing the method.
4. In secondary schools where teachers have multiple classes the other end can be painted. This way, each class set can be easily identified and rouge sticks which end up in the wrong pot rapidly rectified.

Limitations:
1. It enables you as the teacher to choose someone at random, but like any random process, only operates successfully on questions which are whole-class directed. It will not allow for any differentiation of the demand of the question, unless this built-in.
2. Beware of the lollipop thieves. After two weeks of one student's name never being drawn, I became suspicious. On closer inspection I discovered the child had surreptitiously removed their stick in a bid for an easy ride.

3. Consider carefully what happens to the stick after being drawn. If they remain out of the pot then this gives any child a reprieve of having to actively participate once their stick has been picked for around 30 questions. A solution to this is to return them to the pot immediately, in the knowledge that leanings towards an individual will be resolved over the course of multiple lessons. Alternatively returning the sticks every 5 questions is an easy compromise. There is always the option of removing one stick for a short time,   while a student who has had an unfair proportion of the questions. They don't have to know you have done this.

Balls

One clever alternative is to purchase a set of ping pong balls. These can easily be painted using water based paint, ideally four colours with eight balls each. These balls can then be numbered from 1 to 32. Each child is then assigned a number, which when drawn requires them to answer the question.

Benefits

This method of selection has many of the same advantages as the lollipop sticks, with a few additional benefits:

1. Unlike the lollipop method this technique will allow for differentiation, this is why the balls are painted differently. When assigning the numbers you can ensure the most able in the class have numbers which correspond to the same colour, then the next ability group and so on. Now after asking a particularly challenging question you can skew the choice of questestant simply by choosing a yellow ball rather than a red one.

2. The colours also allow you to direct the students when working in groups. Instructing the students to work with another student of a different colour or form a group of four with one of each colour is a quick way of achieving mixed ability groups. Equally, pitting the red and green students against the yellow and blue can encourage some healthy competition.

3. One set will cater for all groups. Having used the lollipop sticks for many years before discovering this idea, I can't stress what a relief this was to me. I have countless lollipop sticks forgotten and neglected at the bottom of a cupboard with the names of students past scrawled on them.

4. Perhaps not seen as a benefit to those on the receiving end of it, however I very much enjoy the endless 'ball' related innuendo that, for me, never grows old.

Limitations:
1. Time is required to make the set. They need to be prepared carefully. I tend to alternate the colours when numbering so as to ensure that all class sizes will be catered for. If balls 1 to 8 are all the same colour a class of 10 would have limited capacity for differentiation.
2. Assigning the numbers to students cannot be done immediately. Although target data and the previous years data may be available to divide up the class, I find I prefer to get to know my class and their abilities before introducing this technique, usually around October half term. In certain circumstances even the target data may not be sufficient. A top set in a core subject is likely to have 30 students all with target grades of A and A* grades.
3. Balls roll off desks in a way that lollipop sticks do not. A paperclip creates a very easy makeshift 'stand' to help prevent this.

Hands Up: Questions to ignite thinking in the classroom

Arbitrary selection

If you aren't a fan of props and craft, using an arbitrary selection system works just as well to identify those questestants. Selecting someone with a birthday in January, an older sister, someone with four pets or who walked to school is a way of diminishing the number to choose from.

Benefits:
1. This is an excellent method to use at the start of the year in order to help you get to know a new class or form group.
2. By filtering into a small group, you are focusing your attention on a random element, meaning all of the class has buy-in, followed by that group; all of which leads to increased attention.
3. It is especially good for questions which you'd expect the majority of the class to be able to answer, so it doesn't ignore right answers from a majority, just the minority who weren't selected as part of your random group.

Limitations:
1. Although this can add a fun element it does add another element to process for the students without progressing the learning at all.
2. There will be a limit to the pace which can be achieved when using this method.

3. You are very much reliant on student buy in. There is scope for those students who were previously ardent cloudholders to suddenly acquire an older sister in a bid to be chosen. Of course the converse may also occur, students absentmindedly forgetting the month of their birth to avoid the spotlight.

Thou shall not accept "I don't know" as a response

What could seem to be quite an innocuous response from the students can, if widely overused, become very destructive in a classroom setting. Students should not be allowed to develop passive resistance to classroom participation. One of the reasons teachers can shy away from 'no-hands up' techniques can be due to fear of this response and the resulting impact on the pace of their lesson.

There are a number of ways to avoid this both on an individual and whole class basis. One method is to regularly use tasks in which, after brief thinking time or paired work, every student is required to give an answer. Allow repetition of answers if need be initially but insist on contributions from every group, pair or individual.

With the individual student develop a routine to handle the "I don't know" answer when it comes following a question. You may not always get a response from the student, however do not just accept the lack of response and move on. There are several ways in which you can acknowledge the response and attempt to rectify it.

Ask the student if it would help if you rephrased the question; this is an opportunity for another student to potentially be used.

Alternatively, another student could be given the same question first, if there are a number of possible answers available. This has the effect of providing some thinking time for the original student, but also models a potential answer before they are required to suggest their own.

The question could be asked to another student, the teacher initially accepting the cry of "I don't know", however the original student then returned to assess the quality or validity of the answer. Here the ever so useful, 'why?' can be employed with free abandon in order to ensure the student doesn't escape with a superficial "Yes he's right."

Consider it may of course be your fault! Have you allowed the students sufficient time to formulate their answer? Think time is important; ask the student if they need a moment to do just that. If you are getting multiple "I don't knows" it may be a good idea to stop and allow some quick paired discussion.

If none of this appears to be working, or if in the interest of pace you do not wish to pause for paired discussion, tell the student you will return to them with the next question. A promise that you must, under all circumstances, keep.

Hands Up: Questions to ignite thinking in the classroom

Thou shalt indulge in wait time

Most questions are answered in less than a second, either by the chosen student or the teacher themselves. In the interest of pace, students are rushing answers and those who have yet to process the question are left wondering what just happened. It should be no surprise to discover that by consciously increasing wait time to 3 seconds for closed questions and 10 for open increases not just the number of students volunteering answers but also the quality of the response (1978 study by Mary Budd Rowe). Students require time to process what is being asked of them, to formulate an answer of good quality.

The same study also found a positive impact if there was increased time between the child's response and the teacher passing a comment on this response. By taking a pause and allowing the students answer to hang in the air for a moment it encourages the students themselves to reflect, add to and amend their own answer. It also allows the other students in the class to form an opinion on the answer. Try taking that pause and watch the hands of others snake upwards, keen to comment.

The benefits of increasing wait time are well documented and easy to see in practice, however, to have the self-discipline to remain quiet will be the challenge for most teachers. Waiting for 10 seconds seems like an easy task however in front of 30 waiting children it can seem like an age. If you really find it a struggle, one tactic is to display a question for discussion on the board but not to address it until later in the lesson or pose a question at the end of the lesson to be picked up in the following lesson.

Try this

Choose a suitably open question requiring a robust and well thought answer. Pose this to your class and wait. Not just for 10 seconds but longer. You will hopefully feel slightly awkward as the class in front at you look to you to choose someone to respond. Wait, ride out the glances and the silence. I like to use the first nervous giggle from a student as my cue to choose someone to answer. How do the responses compare?

Thou shalt employ Carrots and Sticks

There is always a benefit to adding a carrot or stick when questioning, depending on your aim for the question. By carrot, this refers to an incentive for the student to answer more than simply the stock phrase which makes the teacher turn their focus to someone else. By stick, corporal punishment is to be avoided! Instead, try to develop pressure in your students to make their answers count when questioning them. The following are proven strategies to employ if desiring carrots and sticks as a way of improving responses.

Earn the reward

Rewards are always an excellent way to encourage participation and can take many forms. They may be tangible prizes (for example stickers, postcards or even small gifts) but do not have to be. Praise and recognition can be just as effective at encouraging the desired behaviour of the students.

It is worth reviewing what rewards you make available to the students in your classroom but also what the students actually have to do to earn your elusive rewards.

Try some of the following tactics:

State the prize upfront - announcing at the beginning of the starter task that the best quality answer will have postcard sent home will ensure the students focus on the quality of their answers.

Give the students success criteria - what features of their answer will make the answer good quality and worthy of your reward. We eagerly give the students success criteria for written tasks but how readily do we for their verbal contributions?

Bank the reward - give them a reward which will be redeemed later on in the lesson. It could be as simple as being the first to leave the classroom.

Don't underestimate the power of a sticker - A Level classes can be the most eager to earn stickers. Stickers hold a universal appeal and should not be reserved only for the younger students. An inflatable trophy, on to which I could write the reining 'good quality answer' champions name, was extremely popular.

Praise contributions. For some students making the effort to contribute to a lesson, however small, requires substantial effort. If these students are to be encouraged to contribute more, then praise should be given regardless of whether the answer given is correct. Caution must of course be exercised so as not to overly cultivate *cloudholders.*

Encouraging written responses

Many teachers are now 'encouraged' to write comments in pupil books in a variety of pens, colours and styles, either restating the learning objective, or next steps, or targets for the future - sometimes all of these! I wonder if anyone has measured the CWC (Comment Word Count) and found a correlation between a higher number and an impending Inspection?

Questions are a great way to encourage interaction with comments, and are also a way to take the learning further, but without a carrot, what incentive is there to actually answer the question in the comment?

There are a number of things that can be done by you as the teacher to ensure that these written questions are not left wallowing unanswered:

- Ensure that every child has been set a question. If they don't all have to respond to something then it undermines the collective importance.
- Leave a space where the students are required to respond. One useful method is to draw a box into which the students must write their answers.
- Dedicate time to during the lesson to allow the students to respond to the question. If the students are required to give full and detailed answers to your questions then they must be allowed sufficient time to do so.
- Withhold any reward/ merit/ grade/ sticker until the question you have posed has been answered by the student.

Questions posed in the students books not only creates a new level of dialogue between you and the student, it also progresses the learning, as the pupil has to think about their work in more detail (and with a built-in break between production and reflection, which is crucial).

This strategy works incredibly well in all topics, and over time, builds a vivid picture of their understanding in your subject, feeding your assessment of their work.

Try this

Examine what carrots your classroom environment and marking scheme offer as incentives for students. What makes them effective? How could this be improved?

Echo Answers

The fluorescent sticks which are used in CSI to show the trajectory of bullets (to a thumping dance tune) fascinate me in that I often wonder what the same would look like in dialogue terms in the classroom. It often feels like there are simply lines to and from teacher and individual pupils, with very little interaction from pupil to pupil, even in learning pairs.

A similar analogy would be tennis as compared to volleyball. Are we having discrete dialogue with one pupil, then another, or are we encouraging a greater share of co-operative learning in our class, with students interacting and building on one another's responses?

Echoing answers aims to address this. Instead of a student in a pairing blithely sharing what they said in a learning pair, develop an expectation that one person from the pair reports what the other person said. This immediately places a pressure on those in the pair to listen more carefully to what their partner is saying rather than simply waiting for their turn to speak.

It also encourages the more passive of the pairing allowing the other person to speak on their behalf. It gives them something to say which they can't be judged against (since they are simply reporting back) whilst at the same time encouraging them to contribute. Wins all round.

Hands Up: Questions to ignite thinking in the classroom

Thou shalt measure the attention span

A rule of thumb I was taught very early on in my teacher training was the rough gauge of attention span; we were told to consider children's attention spans to be their age in minutes plus one. It's good as a rule of thumb which sadly crashes at around secondary age (I for one cannot concentrate for 29 minutes).

The four year old attention span is of course far less than five minutes; thirty seconds at some points perhaps. Yet, when engaged (books, LEGO, toy adverts), this attention span increases.

The use of questions can help to re-engage this attention span with comfortable ease. It can give an emphasis on refocusing a particular skill, rereading for meaning, or encourage pace in a particularly long depth task.

One skill of a teacher is to tacitly measure the attention span of your class as if they were four year olds. Don't wait until they are off task; instead ensure that they remain on task through questions. One key indicator for me is if the work becomes boring or too hard, pencils need sharpening and bladders need emptying. Building in questions every few minutes provides both a fuel and momentum which can help to avoid this.

Identify which tasks different teaching groups respond to with better attention spans than others, but be aware of lesson admin, where the class is noisily busy but not productively learning. If the task is to stick words around a diagram, ensure that 90% of student time is sticking rather than cutting (which is classic *learning admin*[1]).

Attention spans can of course diminish within a small length of time if something is long-winded or over-complex. Practise shorter questions - if you have to take a breath, it's too long!

Try this:

An engaged attention span can often be referred to as 'flow' - total immersion in a task, so that there is no desire to time-check. What aspects of your subject have you noticed provide opportunities for total immersion? How could you develop these further?

---

[1] A task which the students appear busy but aren't actually learning anything. They are effectively 'noisily busy.'

Thou shalt avoid anchors

An anchor in this sense is a hook to which all answers gravitate toward - anchors can take answers off at a tangent really quickly, and it can be very hard to take the children back to the direction you were hoping they would head.

At its most simple, this can happen when a child makes a wild guess for an answer, and this sidetracks the rest of the class into thinking that they must have been close. How to tackle this takes skill, as you need to undo the anchor that's been made, whilst re-framing the question to something more specific, and at the same time not damaging the confidence of the anchoree!

As an example, imagine you have asked the children where the coldest place is. It's a rubbish question, as it is far too vague, and if you were hoping that the children would suggest Antarctica, and the first person says freezer, you'll discover very quickly that children are more likely to have answers which derive from freezers than what was in your head!

There are two ways to address this, but both require you to take the students closer to the correct answer. The first is to unpick the anchor question, to hold it up for scrutiny, by testing it out with the class. This way they can see that it doesn't fit. This takes the class closer to making a more accurate answer.

The other is to reframe the question, and give a breadcrumb toward understanding - so by giving the children a simple anchor such as holding a globe in your hands when you ask the question about the coldest place.

Closed questions are the most likely to provide inaccurate answers to the children, so be careful to give signposts where possible through judicious phrasing.

It can help in factual answers to give   high and low limits, or narrowing the choices it could be. If you have asked the children for an estimate for 28 x 31 for example, and a child says 60, it would be sensible to round the numbers with the class, so that they have a firmer grasp of the question asked of them.

Offering a pat deflection such as *"not quite"* or *"larger than that"* gives no direct feedback on the accuracy of the answer given. This however tends to be default, and allows anchoring to occur really quickly, so try to avoid this whenever possible.

Try this:

Recognise when you next hear an anchor in an answer, and try where possible to build positive anchors in your questioning repertoire.

Thou shalt make your questions that simple

Are the questions we ask in class simple enough for a four year old to understand? Possibly so, if you are in EYFS, but no question asked of a class should *ever* be difficult to understand. Tricky to break down certainly, as this is a skill we want to encourage at times. Some questions should also be difficult to answer, as this avoids a thoughtless pat response, but questions themselves should, by default, be simple.

Look at Apple as model of refining and stripping back unnecessary detail with a product and place those values against your questions. Does your question need so much concentration that the answer is muddied in the children's heads? If they need to refer to something in front of them, is this innately clear before they get asked the question? Do they even know what type of answer you are expecting them to produce?

One test carried out for dyslexia is where a child is given a growing list of instructions to follow, the test designed to see how many instructions the child can carry in their head before becoming confused and getting things out of order. Is this what we want to happen to our pupils? Do we want them to be overwhelmed by a question so much that they experience 'choke' in their responses?

Pare down your questions as much as possible in order to make it as accessible as possible for your pupils. It is far better that they spend time encoding an answer than decoding your question.

Try this

If no-one responds to a question you ask, is it too difficult to understand? Have you linked two sentences together, or had to draw breath before completing it? Have you allowed sufficient wait time, for the students to process an answer?

Thou shall not ask the same question repeatedly

"How many times do I have to ask the same question?"

The answer - never! If your question isn't understood the first time, is it fit for purpose? We as educators suffer from the "Theory of Knowledge" - that we often assume that our children understand concepts as well as us, and can make the same jumps we are able to achieve as informed adults. By repeating a question, all we are doing is emphasising that they aren't able to make those leaps.

Try to not repeat the same question in the same way. Add details, or reframe it in a way which makes what you are asking more accessible to the children. One way to do this is to assume that the learners can't make the jump you are expecting them to, so signpost which direction you want them to take.

We habitually seek out the same answers using the same phrases - but in order to expand our pupils' literacy across all subjects and disciplines, we need to ensure that they can seek out an answer from many different angles. For that reason, try to go in a totally different direction and, instead of repeating the same question, aim not to make any of your questions the same!

This is almost impossible to maintain, but while you are doing so, it is forcing you to evaluate new ways to ask the same thing - you may even find a better way of phrasing something which works.

Try this

Never repeat the same question in the same way. Slow yourself down, add emphasis and reframe it if possible.

Thou shalt place names with care

Placing a name first or last in a question can have significant benefits and costs, as the following section explains.

Before you read on, consider; how often do you use your pupils' names in questions? Do you err toward names preceding or completing a sentence? Why is this?

Name first

This gets the attention of the person you are asking, but also puts the focus on them, whilst at the same time excluding others from the answering process.

One way to tackle this is to offer a soft coaxing statement in the question to build confidence. For example:

"Chloe, I know you've been exploring rivers. What major types were you able to identify as common around the region we've been exploring?"

This pinpoints them as the questestant, highlights their qualification for giving an answer, then points out exactly the sort of answer you are expecting from them. This is a three beat question, with a lot to take in, so it is best to ask this slowly and clearly. By doing so, you are giving real value to the answer, as the question has been framed for the whole class.

With some questions, you might want to encourage others to think of an answer, even if the question is directed at one specific pupil. One way to do this is to encourage the indication of an answer (I use potato fists - one fist above the other, on the desk), which allows others to join in silently, but without being off-putting in the way a sea of hands can be for some students.

The use of name first questioning is most beneficial for those children with poor attention, as it ensures they are engaged with the question addressed to them. It goes without saying, you should make full eye contact with them when asking it.

Try this

Use the three-beat question format to help build the confidence of your lower achievers. Making them centre-stage, while overtly indicating their ability to answer your question underlines their value.

Name last

"We've explored primary colours, but what would we say are secondary colours, Michael?"

Strictly speaking, asking a question with the name added onto the end is a supplementary question. This is the teaching equivalent of a searchlight on a student/victim, and should be used wisely. If it has been asked because Michael isn't paying attention, it is a question widow, and should be avoided. Instead, address the attention issue, *then* move to the question, as you would (hopefully) then have everybody's attention. Don't waste the opportunity of asking question!

The reason it is often used like this is that a teacher involuntarily scans students when speaking, so it is simple to point out a student who is not with you at the end. Instead, scan *before* you ask the question, addressing any attention issues, then ask. This engages all students with the question, which is the overall aim of your role.

So why might you put a name at the end of a question? Perhaps the best reason to do this is when you can see a student who really wants to answer, especially if they aren't normally so keen. By pinpointing them at the end, you are indicating that they are likely to give the right answer you are seeking. This raises the pressure on them, certainly, but also offers them a strength of your conviction in their reply. Used in this way, putting a child's name last is incredibly powerful.

Try this

Address low-level distraction or wandering attention before speaking to the class, either through non-verbal cues or some other indication. A common mistake, especially for new teachers, is to plough on, speaking and asking questions, hoping that their interesting wisdom will quell the class.

Hands Up: Questions to ignite thinking in the classroom

Slopportunities

There are many small moments in the day when the children aren't involved in active learning. These are really slopportunities, moments when we have the students in front of us, yet not interacting with them in any beneficial way. Given the preciousness of time in our school days, we should really seek out these missed learning moments in our contact time, and get those fresh young brains engaged and thinking for themselves.

This section covers some of these missed opportunities, but there are plenty more from the moment your pupils arrive to the time they leave (and outside of these times too) - consider the learning cracks in your timetable. What could you fill them with?

Lining up questions

Lining up is one activity when the class come together slowly, with the chance of a rich experience presenting it to the teacher on a (queued) plate.

Take this time to ask reflective questions about your core class values, about the school ethos, about the way they present themselves. Give them a hook for a few seconds of inward reflection.

The difficulty with events like lining up is that it is often the usual suspects who appear at the front of the line; those who are closest, most organised or most keen to escape. Turn this to your advantage, and make the questions you ask more inviting for those who often end up near the rear of the line. Create a carrot from questions, not a stick.

Similarly, children often leave in a staggered format. How might you utilise this? Here are some quickfire methods:

Pop Quiz

Quick, simple closed questions as you stand by the door forces the pupils to take their learning outside as they leave your classroom, as well as being a blunt tool to see what takeaways your students have gained from the lesson.

Exit Tickets

These are simple slips with either a question or challenge on them. More common in Secondary Schools than Primaries, they nevertheless work exceptionally well as a tool for measuring impact in a shortened form. Some teachers use these in lieu of a homework slot, while others expect the students to bring them back for the next lesson, as the basis of a starter. Their exit ticket may even be a request for more information on x, or even a question to the teacher.

Mystery Box
A coloured box where students can put in questions during the lesson can be opened up and asked of the students as they leave. A Post-It note given to all pupils can operate in a similar way, with the teacher collecting in the questions put on Post-Its, and redistribute them to the rest of the class. To leave, they must attempt to answer the question.

Board Questions
Write a simple question on the board, and to leave, students have to give an answer to leave. Try and encourage variety rather than repetition. This operates best with the children have some thinking time first.

Try this
Ask a question quietly to the first two lined up in a row, and ask them to whisper back an answer. The quickest formation will follow.

Hands Up: Questions to ignite thinking in the classroom

Registration questions

"When was the last time you were really cold?"
"What did you dream about last night?"
"How many pets do you own?"

Registration is innately necessary and the same time profoundly boring. Mix it up by asking a question to the class each day. The rules I use are that they can't have the same answer as someone else, and that no question is ever repeated.

This activity takes far far longer than registration (which is actually done by counting the empty chairs in class or a quick headcount), but is far richer in terms of dialogue with your class. It encourages everyone to share something of themselves, get them set up for a day when they are expected to contribute in class, and helps in making your classroom dynamic, more sharing and open.

My class love it, and in the times I've been in a rush to take the register, they are insistent on me coming up with a quick question. By making it about them and personal, it offers no intellectual demands yet prompts them to speak up and have a voice. For some of your class, whatever your teaching bells and whistles, this might be the only question they answer with confidence all day. Don't miss this opportunity.

As a side benefit, by starting with your answer, you get to share something of yourself in the classroom, as well as having a gift-wrapped entrance to conversation with every child in your class.

Try this

Take your registration using questions they have to answer at the next opportunity you get. It will take longer, so build this time in somewhere.

Question Widows in books

"What would you change next time?"
"Which was your favourite part of the story?"
"Which other words could use use to describe the ridge?"

There is truly nothing sadder than a question widow, sitting forlornly at the bottom of some work. It's a simple truth, but if there is no purpose or benefit to answering a question, why on earth would we, even as adults, answer it? If the question has been written there for the benefit of a reader other than the student themselves, that is even worse - it's a scorned widow, as it was never intended to be answered in first place!

This is an enormous slopportunity which teachers are regularly guilty of committing. It may seem beneficial to ask a question in their writing, but if the only response expected is just to be read, there is no way of knowing if this will even happen, let alone be taken on board.

As a widow, it is without purpose and a waste of your energy. Worse still, it sends the implied message to the pupils that you are asking empty questions. Extend this practice across your whole lesson, and the message to your students is that only certain things you say have value; in truth, everything you say should have value.

Here then are four quick tips for using questions in comments more effectively:

Force an extension

Ask the student to carry on with the work, showing three examples of x where they can demonstrate something they struggled over in the original piece.

Hold back the reward

Only give a reward if they answer your question. This forces the learning to be the destination rather than the reward. This can be made more effective by creating a space for the response - red boxes work well, as do Avery labels stuck in. Dedicate time at the start of the next lesson for students to respond to your marking. Check that the response has been made and in doing so, emphasise the expectation that they should be answered and completed.

Corridor questions

How many times do we pass students along corridors? Questions which require more than just deep thought or quick Googling are perfect for corridor questions - small challenges which tease the students just enough to energise them into seeking out answers and finding you to get some form of tangible recognition are worth their weight in gold.

Why not set this up as a subject or faculty theme, and see who can pose the best brainteaser for the pupils - with answers revealed at the end (by the pupils of course).

Q and A

Mark these letters clearly in the margin, and create a reflective culture, where you refuse to mark another piece of work until you have an answer next to A! This takes enormous discipline on both parties however - be warned.

Try this

Identify in your marking and teaching if you use question widows or not. Excessive use needs to be tapered to sparingly, if at all.

Questions in display

Display has never been my strong point, yet there seems to be a profusion of emphasis that displays should have questions attached to them. This is explored in the next few pages.

Why ask a question no-one can answer?

There is a growing popularity on displays of putting questions for the audience to answer. The difficulty with this is that there are often various audiences for a display (your class, other classes, parents, SLT, Inspectors), who need different questions.

The key difference between a statement on display and a question is that the latter is a clear call to action - yet this is rarely the case in displays. Decide on a clear call for action - what do you want the audience to take, gain or contribute from the display - and base your questions around this.

The bigger problem though is that often most displays have question widows. Consider the following questions, taken from actual displays:

"Which is your favourite photo?"
"Can you see two matching shapes?"
"How many countries do you know?"

What is the intention of these answers? They are homeless and purposeless. With a small adjustment, each of these can be turned into a question with purpose, and transform

70

your display into something with an intention beyond simply showing good work.

"Which is your favourite photo, and why? Please sign our Gallery Book"

Using a gallery or visitors book makes your display interactive, gives feedback to the children on their photographs, and is a lasting record of the display/achievement.

"Use the pegs to match the shapes."

A tag flap under each shape, and some pegs joined by coloured wool allows those looking at the display to interact with it. It gives your display more viewing time, passes on some learning and is incredibly easy to 'reset.' A really busy teacher (imagine that!) would make a student the official display monitor to reset it for them.

"How many countries do you know? Take our quiz."

This is an easy strategy which spreads the word about your learning, and takes no more effort than photocopying a blanked map of Europe, and placing a photocopy paper box with a slit in it for the answers. This is truly interactive, and can involve many more children than those in your class.

Who is your audience

Deciding who your question audience is helps you immensely if using questions in display. Any display's major purpose should be to enhance, enrich or promote learning, so questions should do the same. To that end, the vast majority of questions on a display should be directed at the children whose display it is. These questions of course will be read by others, so give careful thought to the language - it should be accessible yet relevant. Check your learning intentions for key words to feature.

Teacher Audiences

A display for teachers, such as a visual guide for a new marking process, can benefit from having questions added to it, but this should ideally be backed up with a paper or email version of the questions, in the right order. It is far easier to answer a series of questions for a process than follow a list of instructions.

Inspection Audiences

It seems that these are a necessary evil. A highly-coloured speech bubble with a salient question can tick this box to make the display 'interactive,' but I would highly encourage you to make them truly interactive using ideas suggested elsewhere.

Parent Audiences

If you are asking questions to your parents, these are often questions you'd hope they would echo with their own children at home. Don't leave this to chance - why not take a photo of the display, then list the questions for the children to answer together with their parents? These can then be displayed underneath or around the display - and there is no better incentive for involvement from the parents than seeing all the other responses on the display!

Try this

Audit the nearest three displays to you. If there are question widows, ask how you might alter them to become more active. If there are no questions, consider how you might use questions in those displays. The average work of art has a viewing time of six seconds. Can you triple this for a display?

Building a curriculum pathway

I sat in on a violin demonstration recently in an assembly, and near the end, there was a moment for questions. One question asked what the bowstring was made from, and the answer came back it was horsehair. The children were off - the next six questions were all about this - do they kill the horse to take it off, is the horse alive when it happens, why horses and not squirrels (genuinely).

You can never fully predict the tangents that the children will take you on, but their interests in questions will show their curiosity with innate speed and clarity. Do we allow students enough time to ask questions of interest? More importantly do we give them enough time to even explore their own interests?

Questions can build a curriculum pathway if they are taken on board and considered. A curriculum built around the natural interest of the student is one which will engage, excite and inspire them. This isn't to hand over the reigns, but to ensure they feel part of the journey. Questions can be the key to this process.

As with any curriculum, begin with your objectives and end goal in the forefront. I am not advocating handing over the reigns, more giving the children ownership of the path. Recent research on Minecraft has for example shown that eleven-year-olds are able to digest College-standard instructions and writing about the game. Why? They have a strong interest and thus, enormous buy-in. By using questions and the pupils' own interests to allow a shape and direction for the objectives, the path they follow is

74

comfortable, familiar, yet can also be challenging and achieve your objectives.

If this makes you feel uncomfortable, begin a new topic by introducing the topic title, and ask them to write down all the questions they would like to have answered by the end of the topic. Doing this on a piece of large sugar paper encourages a wider range of questions to be asked. Have these displayed in your classroom somewhere.

It is often surprising how many of the questions get answered by the end of the topic anyway, but as the learning progresses, tick off any questions as they are addressed. This helps to reinforce the impact of the lesson, as well as acknowledging a level of ownership for the students. It's incredibly exciting and rewarding for both the teacher and the pupils to see this pathway revealing itself, and any unanswered questions at the end are excellent for 'next steps' opportunities too.

Try this

Before planning a new topic, ask the prospective students three questions they'd like answered from this topic, and build the topic around answering these questions, either as part of the lesson itself, or as further exploration (based on your teaching).

Reading questions

My own daughter Daisy was delighted when she got her first reading book, but was soon filled with scorn when she discovered, quite early on, that there was the same word on every single page. She raced through it, tears in her eyes, and closed it with dejected completion. We opened it again, and I asked her a few questions about what was going on with each new page. The words of this book were really secondary to the story, which could be true for every reading book if it is serving us well.

Reading Schemes are a strange beast; parents love them, publishers build empires on them and yet teachers often get frustrated with them. Yes, they may scaffold reading, but many parents see it as a race to complete the colour/series/set as quickly as possible.

The race for pace can be delayed by encouraging the asking of questions. These can be about recap, review, the characters, scene, setting or action. They should aim to let the story become a story rather than a series of words the children race through in order to get to the next book. At the same time, they shouldn't be onerous or diminish any pleasure a reading book gives.

A Key Stage One teacher I know expects books to last one week, and that the children should be able to answer questions about the story successfully at the end of this week. It creates a culture of immersion rather than speed with reading, and with the added meaning, long-term pleasure can be built upon.

A highly-recommended book for younger children is "You Choose" by Pippa Goodhart and Nick Sharratt. It is entirely without story, and very few words, yet will last upwards of half an hour each time you read it. It is the most incredible book for encouraging conversations, and is excellent for developing questioning skills with books, so is a great training ground.

(Stupid Dad Awards: I once sat next to my son Dylan with a story book based around a farm. "What sort of animals do you think will be on the farm?" He turned to me, with a deadpan face and said, "Just read the story." That was me told!)

Try this:

At the next opportunity you have to read a book to a child, ask a question on every page. It will change the dynamic of the story and the reading experience for you both.

Hands Up: Questions to ignite thinking in the classroom

Students asking questions

Student Questions are the lifeblood of curiosity. Their questions matter, and should be encouraged, directed and explored as much as possible.

This section explores the different ways students ask questions, how to build these opportunities

Grouping Dynamics

The environment a student is in can determine the quantity and quality of their questioning skills. Clearly, good models of questioning are essential, so can the way the dynamic is built around the pupils help this process?

Groups

If your pupils are working in groups, it is really effective to target a question at those groups specifically. We are all aware of the dangers of groups, in that there is almost always one vocal spokesperson, and they speak for the group as a whole. Instead, frame the question in such a way that someone from that group is either targeted, or choose someone specifically from the group. Acknowledge whether or not they are answering on behalf of the others or not - this really matters, and if necessary, validate this with them!

Mute

Sometimes there are just those eager, confident children whose hands are upright in a rigor mortis fashion. They are golden for Inspections, but can end up being quite draining if you are seeking fresh voices. One strategy is to put them on mute! This may seem cruel, but actually recognises their positive contribution, while also allowing others to have a voice and not be intimidated by those expert cloudholders. This can be used lightly, but with confidence, and can change the dynamic quickly.

Rationing

For the perennial cloudholders in class, those who are most eager to answer any question at all, giving a limit to questions they can answer via a Ration Card or some form of token (LEGO cubes for example) forces them to be more judicious in their choices, which in turn allows more questions to be answered by others in the class.

Building questions into answers

Questions provide a neat framework for an answer, but this is something which is often missed by teachers. If you are getting frustrated by your students giving one word answers in written tasks, simply making them include the question in their answer will help them to be more clear in their explanation and understanding. To carry this out most effectively, we must employ that old friend, *why*.

Look at this example, without the question wrapping:
"What did Shackleton's crew eat when first marooned?"
"Husky dogs and seals."

With the question enclosed in the answer:
"Shackleton's crew ate husky dogs and seals"

Upgrade these answers with a silent *why*. This sits between their answer and a further detail, and gives you an almost effortless fuller answer.

Behind the scenes:
"Shackleton's crew ate husky dogs and seals"
<why>
"It was all they could eat"
<why>
"Nothing else could live there"
<why>
"Antarctica was inhospitable and virtually uninhabitable."

Final answer:

"Shackleton's crew ate husky dogs and seals, as there was no other natural source of food in the inhospitable Antarctic environment."

Note that both answers are correct, and come from the same pupil, with the same knowledge. Based on the answer alone though, who are we likely to think has more confidence in their knowledge of Shackleton?

Developing answers by using the question in them, and expanding them using *why* enhances the children's ability to critically respond to a query, and it is never too early to start this, even orally.

Try this

If you are tired of getting one word responses for a sentence answer, ask the student to wrap their answer in the question.

Here is the answer, what's the question?

This strategy works brilliantly as a lesson or topic starter or plenary, and is deceptively clever in that it uses questions as a form of assessment to the pupil's knowledge. This is a particularly effective technique to employ in Maths, although there is no reason why it shouldn't work well in other subjects too.

By putting an answer on the board, you are immediately giving the students a focus to work back from. They will have to work backwards to a question, which although unusual, is rather a safe path to travel (depending on the question!).

This is a very clever way of adding differentiation with your class, in a quick and effective manner. If you were using the number 14 as your "*this is the answer*" statement, here are some ways to differentiate with ease:

"Can anyone give me a question using decimals?"
"The next question must use subtraction."
"Who can create a question with two fractions?"
"How about a question with three fractions? Is that even possible?"

In each of these example questions, you are testing a specific skill, and so can use this as a rough tool for guiding areas of secure knowledge (by their response rate) as well as areas they are less confident in providing an answer.

It is also a useful technique in encouraging questioning skills with your students. They have many to answer, but only rarely get the opportunity to create their own questions.This is a key skill in establishing how a question is actually designed.

Several teachers now begin a lesson with an image, word, extract or answer in some form, to encourage more questions from the students.

Try this

Whatever your subject, start with an answer on the board, and ask the students to find the question.

Phone in your answer

Asking pupils to 'phone in' their answer to a question avoids them using any prop such as whiteboard work or their books. It encourages them to use more effective language in their answer, and forces them to be more detailed than they might normally be. Put simply, they have to speak their answer through without any props.
The advantages of this are that, over time, the quality of their verbal communication will grow, since they will have to explain everything orally rather than using assistance.

A good example of this is having them explain a punctuation rule, with the other students recreating their instructions on individual whiteboards. They (and you) can see at a glance if the concept has been explained with enough clarity for the other children to produce a 'working' version.

There are of course times when it is beneficial, necessary even, for the students to use examples, point to parts of the whiteboard or hold up laminated cards, but by emphasising the power of an oral answer, you are underlining the vitality of good communication.

It is also a good skill to develop as a teacher. I once spent a week in a new classroom teaching Computing without an overhead projector. It made me much more effective as a verbal instructor than ever before; sometimes, the screen counterpart can be a lazy cousin of teaching. By using language to explain your point, students (especially those with props in front of them) are able to better focus on what you are saying rather than what you are doing.

Try this

Have the students 'phone in' an answer in your next session.

Rhetorical questions

"How long do I need to wait?"
"Surely everybody understands?"

The use of a rhetorical question in the classroom is a powerful tool if used the right way. In its simplest form, it is clarifying your thinking to the class in overt manner. The point is though, if the groundwork has already been carried out in class, what purpose does a rhetorical question have?

By changing it to an actual question, you get to unpick what is *assumed* and discover if your students have *understanding*. In the above rhetorical questions, changing these to statements can have far greater impact, in a very visible way.

"I can see Jamie is ready" can have far greater influence in a classroom than the frustrated and generalist *"how long do I have to wait?"* - surely you as a teacher should not have to wait any time at all, yet you are almost giving the children permission to take their time without any clear model to build upon. By using one student as the behaviour pedestal, it defines the expectations for the other students. This is classic positive reinforcement which can be easy to forget in a busy classroom environment.

Likewise, *"Does everybody know the next step to take?"* is a far greater measure of understanding than *"Surely everybody understands?"* - it works as a quick filter of those students who need to be put back on course or not, and again is an indication of expectation rather than frustration. It helps you as a teacher which students or areas of the classroom need your attention, and quickly, as no progress can be made without your intervention either directly or indirectly. You should however be aware that directing a question at a whole class but only hearing one response can only give a small indication of their group understanding; in this situation, a rhetorical question seeks out those who need guidance, rather than those who don't.

So when should you use rhetorical questions? They work best when used for explicit clarity which demands the student consider them independently, as they can emphasise the classroom intentions more clearly.
"Everyone has remembered to underline their title, haven't they?"

They are excellent as a format of organisational reminder, but they can also be used to provoke; David Rogers gave an excellent lesson where students were encouraged to challenge the statement "Surely Africa caused Ebola?" using this as the launch for a more thorough (and thus, deeper) examination of the Ebola epidemic of 2014/2015.

Avoid a climate where students feel they have been given a 'right' to simply call out, damaging your classroom behaviour expectations.

Try this
Be more conscious of using rhetorical questions when there are more effective questions to suit your aim at that point in the lesson.

Vagueness develops intrigue

Another strategy to employ is to keep your aim a secret, then reveal it through questions from the children. This is discovery inquisition, rather than discovery learning, but is hugely effective at making the learning focus incredibly apparent. Conversely, by introducing this through vagueness, it makes it more tangible for the children.

The best way to explain this strategy at work is by using an example of a lesson I was teaching on landlocked countries in Europe. Rather than stating the lesson objective, I put on the board a political map of Europe, with the names removed. The children had to name a country in Europe (and locate it, if confident enough). I would point it out, then give out a number. This was the number of countries that surrounded the chosen country. The children had to identify what the numbers related to on the map.

This type of activity captures their imagination, gets them engaged, and also improves their filtering skills, as they have to consider options through trial and error. This strategy is not as transferable as others, and yet it is worth exploring to liven up one of the more dull objectives you might have to deliver.

It has been described as discovery inquisition, since the nature of inquisitiveness is to desire more information. By fuelling that desire, while also solved a purpose, we are helping students to become more curious.

Many schools require teachers to state their learning intention on the board - by building an activity around this intention it underlines, rather than subsumes it.

Try this

For your next lesson, don't write down your learning intention on the board to tell the class; instead work out some way for the class to work it out.

"Please explain that to my four year old."

My friend Alan trains negotiation skills with some of the largest companies and brands in the world, and he is regularly surrounded by high level managers and directors who are able to cloak waffle in very verbose management-speak. He uses the question above to cut to the quick with ease, and I have unashamedly stolen this concept from him.

What this question does is encourage the students to fillet their response to the simplest and clearest answer possible. This isn't the easiest skill for children to develop, so needs support and encouragement. Replaying a response in four year old terms helps the children to scaffold future responses. What we are really enhancing here is a level of articulacy that strips away layers, rather than builds them up, which is sought more often.

This question is also incredibly useful in training days, staff meetings and other adult learning sessions. The best training for me is when a trainer is able to explain a new concept with such perception it seems incredibly obvious and makes you question why you never thought of it before! Surely the sign of a good teacher, who rather than joining the dots for you, makes you develop this skill independently.

Using this question with both adults and students helps to retain understanding and enhance clarity of thought.

Try this

At the next training session, be brave enough if you are confused to use this question - an excellent trainer will be able to answer you with ease, even with the most complex of topics.

Silent debates

This is an idea with a very difficult provenance to ascertain, but I liked the idea so much, I braved it for a lesson during an inspection. It was new for both myself and the children, but lent itself so well for the lesson aim, I couldn't resist.

A silent debate is when you offer a question on a large piece of paper, and the children silently debate it by writing down their answers. They are allowed to challenge other responses, ask questions, and expand ideas, but just using pencil and paper.

It works amazingly well, and any fears about those less literate children being unable to access the activity are generally unfounded. Conversely, I've found that they are more drawn into the task than you would expect, and contribute well. The pace is theirs, and they are able to go in their own direction, not in a strictly linear fashion as might normally be the case.

A silent debate is a very powerful way of exploring questioning in a format which is different to normal, and goes off in ways you might not expect. It also helps refine the children's written question skills, which is never a bad thing either.

The resulting sheets from a silent debate can be used in a display, for further work, as an assessment piece, or even photocopied for evidence.

There are several online alternatives to a silent debate, such as Padlet, which allow students to contribute from a variety of sources, but there is a richness to an active, physical procedure like *Silent Debates* that is hard to recreate in an online environment.

Try this

Near the end of a topic, explore whether using a Silent Debate would suit an assessment of the learning covered

Encouraging "Why?"

Tangents can be tricky to manage, especially if you are the sort of teacher with an incredibly low boredom threshold. The "why?" question, which is as genetically imprinted in children as the desire to request completing any project title in 'Bubble Writing,' has enormous value in any classroom. It *demonstrates curiosity* and *seeks clarification* - the two greatest skills desired in a classroom.

Tough question: Do you encourage "*why?*" in your classroom? Are you the sage, the learning hero, with all answers contained within, or do you genuinely want the children to challenge and question you?

An easy win for testing this is to give each child a WHY card (a card with WHY printed on it) at the start of every lesson. Their aim is to ask the question and hand in their card by the end of the lesson - your aim is to avoid anyone giving in their card. Watch the classroom dynamic change!

Once they have mastered WHY card, introduce the BECAUSE card too, and have the children involved in responding to why. By explaining their understanding, this can help to underscore and secure it further.

The use of *why* as a secondary, follow-up question is also an easy win for developing greater thinking skills, since it forces justification and the defence of an idea or concept.

One way to extend this is by exploring Blooms Taxonomy with your class. Share the framework with the students, and indicate to them where you would like their questions and answers to be within this framework. Defining a boundary helps them to focus more clearly on your intention, as well as allowing you to differentiate effectively.

Try this

Print a page of WHY cards and BECAUSE cards, and leave one word of each on every pupil's desk at the start of a lesson. This is question dynamite!

Why do they ask questions?

This may seem a very strange aspect of teaching to consider, as 'they just do' seems to cover it quite well! It would be a strange environment if the children never asked a single question, but the reality is that they ask hundreds a day, so what are these questions, and more importantly, why do they ask them? Indeed, what is our desire for them to even ask questions in the first place, and is it worth spending time making them better at asking questions?

This is something I have considered and believe that questions children ask can fall into three broad categories; clarity, curiosity and procrastination.

Clarity

These are really important, as they flag up a desire to complete a task, but they are missing key information to do this. Clarity is a vital skill in any way of life, but especially in learning, and the desire for clarity is a child indicating that they don't know what to do next in order to progress. This isn't a fault, but will help guide you against the very real danger of the 'Theory of Knowledge' which is a theory suggesting that teachers presuppose knowledge with a student which is greater than that which exists!

How often as teachers have we been surprised that students should just 'know' what we are asking them to do? From a Primary perspective, this is best seen through the repeated reminder to use capital letters and underline titles - despite reminding them every single lesson.

The key takeaway here is that even in a lesson on capital letters, these can be forgotten, since the children are juggling all kinds of inputs and outputs, so a constant reminder is essential to keep the children on task with your objective. Clarity from one child in my mind highlights that perhaps three or four more children are seeking the same clarity but haven't (yet) asked.

Make your expectations and instructions as explicit as possible, and if someone seeks clarification, feed this clarification back to all of the class. It helps to underline something for those who aren't lost, and realigns those who are. Both the instructions and the expectations of the task should be really clearly defined for the students in order for them to both follow and and deliver on these.

For those like a supporting acronym, PRIME is an excellent framework to deliver clarity. This is especially useful for student teachers and NQTs, who often know their aims for a task but struggle to convey these most effectively to their students. It helps to share PRIME with the students on initial use, so they can challenge missing aspects of the framework as they are explained.

PRIME stands as follows.
P - Presentation format; paragraph, notes, drawing?
R - Resources required;
I - Input; is this done individually, pairs or groups
M - Minutes given to prepare/research/complete
E - Evaluation; who and how will this be done?

These do need exploring further depending on the group you are working with. How will the students be required to present the task? Will they be required to feedback verbally or in their books? If so, how will this be presented? What stationery will be required? Where will they get their information from? How will the task be marked? How will they receive their feedback, and in what format will this take place? Consider all these questions when delivering PRIME, and include regular questions you get asked.

Curiosity

In some instances, this can be the best type of question to be asked by the children, the panacea of learning, and yet will often take you off-task temporarily. Wahey! Off-piste learning is one of the most exciting areas of learning, as you aren't sure where it will lead, yet is innately satisfying and rewarding (but possibly not ideal just before exams!). Curiosity is likely to come from one source and not be shared, yet is really interesting to explore.

Some teachers like to offer a place for curiosity in their classroom such as a Wonder Wall. This is a great way for children to share their questions and interests with others, perhaps in the hope that someone else will share this interest.

It is however essential we feed this interest as much as possible. Curiosity is the metaphorical door wide open to a mind, with hands outstretched. Project-based learning, personal assignments and the (much-derided) discovery learning play a key role in building upon curiosity if your planning cannot accommodate it.

Research suggests that discovery learning isn't the most effective or efficient format of learning, yet real-life experience would suggest that while it isn't the most efficient, it can be the most embedded form of learning.

Procrastination

There are of course questions which operate as a form of deliberate learning delay - "*can I go to the toilet?*" being the most common and classic (especially at Primary level). We can get frustrated with procrastinating questions, or we can unpick them and explore what the particular hump is which the child is at, in order to get them going again. The next time a child offers a procrastinating question, delve quickly into their work and see what is creating this hump, and offer a quick solution.

Children can use questions in a divisive way at times, especially with new or inexperienced teachers. They can ask questions repeatedly to delay starting work, or ask over-complex questions of the teacher, to create tangents. All teachers need to develop strategies to address these issues of behaviour management, and their best practices for preventing questions from necessarily taking up learning time. Teachers can over time enable lazy learners by pandering to these questions, and this is written about in more detail elsewhere in this book.

Procrastination is a strategy to avoid either work itself, or work which is too challenging to be carried out immediately - so learn to identify quickly the students which fall into either of these camps, and look at the strategies below to ensure you are delivering the best response to put that child back on track as quickly as is possible.

The most common in my classroom practice is when they have exhausted their energy, enthusiasm or creativity. Identifying these and offering a quick fix is the best way to put the pupil back on course. Here are some quick tips for these three problems:

Energy - do something else for a minute. This is ideally something completely different, but can be as simple as 'read through your last three comments from me,' 'count the number of verbs you have used in that last paragraph' or even 'sharpen your pencil.'

While a brain break maybe seen as Accelerated Learning waffle, research indicates that sometimes our brains need something else to do in order to process another thing internally.

Enthusiasm - This is easy to solve, and is a two-step process which takes seconds. First, praise something they have done well, however small this may be. Secondly, and this is more rarely used but essential, have them actively find something they are pleased with in their work. If need be, get them to underline it!

This tackles enthusiasm in two ways; first it underlines that they are doing well in your eyes, and secondly it emphasises their own personal success in the task. This small act can often be the spark which reignites their fire.

Creativity - Again, this is easy to solve, since you are surrounded by curiosity in the classroom. I tend to solve this in one of two ways; magpie another idea or solve a problem. Ask the child to have a look at three other people's work, and grab an idea from them which they can bring back to their own work.

The other way to make creativity blossom is to ask the children to solve a problem which involves a creative solution - usually through (you guessed it) a question!

Often, it is best to lead with a *why* question, as it forces an explanation rather than an answer. "*Why is the main character so scared?*" is a far better way to relaunch creativity than "*what is the main character thinking?*"

Delivering Confident Answers

Ah, the High Rising Terminal, or Australian inflection as it is better known (by me probably). Almost as frustrating as the excessive overuse of 'like' when not necessary (I involuntarily throw both my arms in the air whenever I hear this in class to signpost its use), it is used by children who aren't fully confident or committed to their answer.

Sometimes a question is answered with a question (*"Is it 14?"*), and at other times an answer is given with deliberation, hesitation or the inflection (*"14?"*). One teacher's standard response to these is, "*are you asking me or telling me?*" One skill we must seek to build is the ability to answer with confidence, but also to hazard guesses when appropriate.

One solution is to encourage the use of different hands up for different responses. The best method is the right hand up for an answer child is confidently *right* about, and the left hand up for an answer they feel is *left* missing something. As a teacher, you can then easily choose a child who you want to deliver the correct answer, or select a child who is often uncertain but regularly correct, and build their confidence. At a glance, you can measure degrees of confidence or doubt, without putting any response under undue pressure.

RAG cards could also be used - holding a green for a confident answer, amber for unsure, and red for an answer which they believe is wrong but can't identify why.

It is worthwhile having students practise what the delivery of a confident answer actually sounds like. You can clearly hear hesitancy in a voice, and instructing students to give a clear confident answer in a positive, upright and assertive manner makes a huge difference to their general confidence too.

Try this

Identify the next high-rise terminal used in your classroom and take the opportunity presented to develop a stronger answer.

Building questioning confidence

Why don't some children ask or answer questions? We all have cloudholders, those children whose hands are up for everything, but working out why some children don't ever ask or answer questions is much harder to solve. Here are some thoughts and possible solutions.

Doubt

Fear of being wrong is crippling and this is exhibited in daily adult life, when the consequences are more serious, yet tend to be less public. The next time you are in a large group where people are expected to contribute, study the extreme discomfort of some people. Their reticence to say anything is often a fear of being wrong, and I say this as someone who is generally happy to speak up publicly - I'm terrified of being wrong, so would rather not contribute unless I'm pretty certain.

The US Marines operate on a 70% certainty level - that is, in a live operation, they can't hope to know all the facts about a situation, so examine everything they have to go on, and proceed on a 70% certainty, knowing that 30% is unaccountable until they are in the situation itself. I'd suggest that we often answer questions using a much higher certainty level, such is our fear of being wrong. Who wants to feel humiliated in public after all?

One way to address this is to remove the fear of being wrong, and offer instead praise at the attempt. Demonstrating the right path or the closeness to the right answer is often a brilliant way of addressing this. Phrases such as *"you are on the right lines"* or *"you are incredibly close, look again at the numbers,"* offer praise and guidance in one neat response, whilst not dismissing the efforts of the child for contributing. It is also really important to praise participation and not simply those who get the right answers, as this emphasises that participation is an essential and vital part of the learning process.

It is important however not to go too far the the other way. Students still need to know their answer is wrong, and should not be in any doubt of this (or else you are allowing them to have an error mistakenly reinforced). One strategy to employ is to thank them for their contribution.

I sometimes give out two verbal praises at the end of a lesson for the two people who have contributed the most - this is at my discretion and often targets both the person who has been right, and the child who has actively had a go, whether right or wrong.

Complacency

Imagine being in a pub quiz with a team of brilliant general knowledge buffs. They know everything, and as the evening proceeds, you find yourself contributing less and less, safe in the knowledge that you'll probably be wrong anyway and your team is likely to win.

In a class situation, the same can happen, and this can either be a forced complacency (*"others will know more than me"*) or relaxed complacency (*"why bother putting my head above the parapet?"*). Both need to be tackled, and this is when you can utilise targeted questioning and the 'name first' technique to quickly identify a temporary expert. Careful, directed praise can help alleviate forced complacency, and naming addresses the latter.

Shyness

There are introverts in every class, and I'd suggest that if you grouped some extroverts together, some would turn into introverts simply because of this situation - a good examples of egos at war.

There are some children who are simply too shy to speak up in class; who for them, the attention of everyone looking or listening to them is far too much to bear. You can of course make every effort to make the environment they are in as unthreatening as possible, but what else is possible?

Taking the idea of a group to a more primal level, what environment could you produce where they *feel* like an extrovert? Is there an area in which they perceive themselves to be an expert or in control? Are you able to engineer it so that they have the confidence to lead or be in charge of questions?

This isn't a simple task, but if you look for an area you feel they are able to blossom in, develop a way in which they can ask or answer questions in this environment, and overly praise their contributions. This is a challenge, but one which over time produces a high level of reward if you are able to build confidence over this aspect of shyness.

There are some occasions when you can have a whole class suffer from a shyness to contribute, often at the start of the day. Adults are the same; count the number of contributions at the start of a training day compared to the middle. Some quick fire closed questions work well to warm up the class. Get them speaking out, and quickly.

A caveat: some children don't respond to certain teachers - this is simply a fact and whatever you do is unlikely to change this. That isn't to say you shouldn't try. My teaching style is lively, upbeat and fast-paced - it really doesn't suit quieter children, so I try to temper this when I am supporting rather than teaching directly, by using a slower and quieter voice, and leading with questions as much as possible, putting children at their ease rather than making them feel they need to compete.

I'll be brave and say my teaching style suits 90% of my class, but that makes me work much harder for the 10% who may find it a difficulty to work within. that 80% are the easy wins, but the final 10% are where you earn your teaching stripes, in my mind!

Redirecting and distracting Individuals

Without doubt, particularly in secondary schools, teachers will utilise questioning to distract those prone to misbehaviour. This can work successfully, however be warned to use this in moderation. Deploying this too regularly can have detrimental consequences both to the individual you are attempting to keep on task but also for the wider class.

In order to avoid the student becoming a question junkie and the rest of the class becoming demoralised, use this student frugally. Avoid throwing closed, skinny questions their way, instead give them a challenging question. Give them a question which requires a substantial answer, an opportunity for the student to feel a sense of achievement. Give them an opportunity to provide you with an answer which you can refer back to later in the lesson.

Deliberate Distractions

On occasion students may use questions in order to deliberately distract from the lesson. In many cases this is harmless and merely requires a reiteration of the expectations. There may be occasions however where one student, or a group of students ask questions in an attempt to undermine the teachers authority. It is easy in these circumstances to take this as a personal attack and become flustered.

114

If you are a new teacher it can be a nerve wracking experience to come up against a student who questions you. It is a new type of questioning that you are unprepared for, questioning of your personal skills as a teacher, your knowledge base of the curriculum, of the exam board or of the workings of the school. It is a type of questioning that, if you become the victim of, you will never forget.

A perfect illustration of this is the tale of Nicola, now an experienced teacher she will never forget the top set year 9 group in her NQT year who made her question herself to the extent that she nearly gave up her chosen career path.

It began slowly and was difficult to pinpoint. Questions about her experience first, how long have you been teaching Miss? Is this your first job Miss? Have you taught this before? She found these difficult to answer but didn't consider these to be inappropriate questions and could understand why they might occur to a child. She'd also been asked them before by other students. What made the difference was that Peter asked these questions publicly; he asked them not to hear the answer but to see her response. He was also relentless. Every lesson he would question Nicola as a professional, frequently quoting other teachers back to her who, through his spin appeared to contradict what she'd said.

Peter was an intelligent and articulate student, who ably led the revolution against Nicola's command. He quickly altered the dynamic of my classroom such that he was in in the position of power. She dreaded her lessons with that group and the relief when those two hours a week were over was palpable.

Nicola learnt through trial and error how to deal with these questions and now laments that she cannot go back and offer support and guidance to her 22 year old self. She has not, however since allowed herself to be in that position again. When reflecting on the experience Nicola cites her biggest mistake was allowing Peter to have the floor. If he were to ask his questions individually she would have found it a nuisance but what had the profound effect on her was the audience. Every response she gave prompted her to anxiously scan the faces of the other students to watch them choose their side. The experienced teacher she has become would now bat his questions away with, "we can discuss that after class", and would wave his hand down with a, "now is not the time". He was an intelligent boy and in his case, it pains Nicola to admit, he required more challenge than she was providing. She have since learnt that this sort of student can easily be addressed through the use of challenging tasks and questions. Ultimately Nicola needed to plan her lessons better to challenge him academically.

Nicola's next error stemmed from her limited acting skills. With other classes she quickly developed a highly positive, confident and overenthusiastic teaching persona, however Peter sowed the seed of doubt. With that class her armour was chipped and she floundered publicly. When asked questions her body language and tone of voice gave away her insecurities. There were so many of his questions she didn't have the answers to give.

Nicola still gets asked questions to which she doesn't have an answer however she now has no qualms about admitting this. It is not a failure to have to double check details of the exam board requirements or dates of exams. Now with the confidence of experience Nicola will use this as a modelling opportunity. She will show the students where to find the examination board website and the details of the specification.

The final lesson Nicola learnt was to be absolutely clear with her instructions. Much of her frustration was due to the feeling of helplessness. She could see the disruption Peters questions were causing but felt she could not challenge his behaviour; after all, how could she reprimand a student for asking a question? This was Nicolas fault. He was disrupting the lesson, yet at no point had she said to the class that they should complete a task independently or should only ask questions about the task. Had she made this clear, any question not about the work would be inappropriate and could be challenged. I'm pleased to report that Nicolas experience with Peter didn't prompt her to leave the profession. She learnt from her experience and has developed into confident and effective teacher.

There are also students who ask these questions in an attempt to seek reassurance. In a large secondary school where students may have had multiple teachers during their time at the school they wish to establish if you can be trusted. These students wish to know that you are familiar with the assessment materials and exam board requirements. They can often be appeased through sharing the big picture. Make it clear what they are learning and how that links to the wider topic and ultimately how they will be assessed, and these questions are likely to dry up.

Hands Up: Questions to ignite thinking in the classroom

Questioning For Progress

Can questions lead progress? Can they even initiate it?

Progress in minute steps has become something of a dirty word in recent times, bated by OFSTED as being essential to be witnessed in class, and defended as being to hidden to be seen by teachers.

Yet progress can be made, and is made, regularly when a careful and incisive question is made by a teacher. You can witness a sea change of understanding with a carefully-phrased question or prompt. This section explores the potential for progress using questions.

Talk time

There is much online conversation about the amount that a teacher should talk in class - from mostly to never! If truth be known, there should be a balance according to the type of lesson and the point at which you are in a topic - a rough guide would be mostly teacher at the start of a topic, mostly pupil by the end. As one Inspector told me, *"if we can't hear the children speaking about their learning, all we can measure is the teacher talking."*

Likewise, how much should we question students is on the same scale. The first part of a topic or lesson should have enough questions to spark thinking and draw the children in. By the end, they would ideally have enough inspiration, and the tools to help them, to be asking the questions, if at all.

Hopefully, the questions they ask at the end of a topic are either to themselves, or related to how they can take this topic forward, how they can connect it to other topics and subjects, and which tools they would use to do so. The ultimate aim of learning should be to generate questions internally, and know how best to explore them.

The end of lesson or topic questions a teacher gives should be short, direct and focused on assessment - that is, next steps for the pupils. This is explored elsewhere in this book. The way to view this is to imagine you are in a car heading toward a large tower. You might ask about the tower as you get closer, comment on it as you pass, and question what you saw as it disappears into the distance. In this sense, questions follow a pattern:

interrogation - affirmation - confirmation

(As an aside, the discussion about talk time is given value in my head when I adjust it slightly to 'walk time' - how much I walk or not in a lesson is directly relevant to the way I am teaching, what I am teaching and how far along we are. To create a fixed measure on walk time is both restricting and ridiculous!)

Try this

Track the number of questions you ask in a single lesson, and their distribution over that time. Mark on a line teacher-directed and pupil-directed time, and using the audio, indicate how many questions you ask each minute. What do you notice about your questioning habits?

Thunks

"What colour is Thursday?"
"Is a pen without ink broken?"
"Is an abandoned car parked?"

These are a genre of question created by Ian Gilbert, aimed to provoke thought, discussion and even dabbling in philosophy through the discussion you can have with students by asking one.

Thunks are a great opportunity to give the children a chance to discuss and debate their viewpoints, as well as defending other opinions. The safety of there being no right answer offers a huge freedom and flexibility to the children's discussions - it is liberating for them to express themselves in a school environment where their perspective is valued higher than simply seeking out the right answer.

Although Ian's book is great, these are questions which the children can generate quite easily without much help. It allows them to think creatively, explore ideas and concepts which no-one would naturally be right or wrong.

During a unit on research skills, one Year 5 class I taught had to generate unGoogleable questions - questions where Google didn't have a ready answer. My favourite from a student was "Can a hippo learn to backflip?" - unqualified GENIUS!

Try this

Have your children create some thunks, then debate them in class!

Interrogation for explanation

"Why are you doing that?"
"What happens next?"
"What might you change next to improve the flow?"

This is a questioning strategy where the search for an answer is reflective rather than regurgitative - the student really has to consider the question rather than grab the stock answer (if available) from their memory.

This is best done working either with one student or a small group. By watching their writing, design or progress, and questioning them as they carry this out, you are admittedly interrupting their flow, but also steering them and making them take a more considerate stance - it is the equivalent of holding the handlebars of a child learning to ride, and giving small left and right adjustments to keep them heading in the right direction.

This questioning strategy is better than modelling, as with that technique, the children are echoing your guide - with *Interrogation for Explanation*, you are drawing them on, so they are taking the lead (with your guidance) - it is far more effective, but very time-intensive. The biggest benefit is that because the feedback is immediate, you can see the changes straight away. It's enormously satisfying.

One way to carry this out is to set all the students a depth task - something which demands their fully independent attention, then take students one or two at a time for an intensive 'learning clinic' - the feedback is enormous and you are able to witness adjustments as they work in a level you would not get with marking, or distance feedback as it might be called in this context.

Much of the problem with marking is that it operates like a post mortem on an underlying fault or deficiency, rather than tackling any difficulties at source. *Interrogation for explanation* addresses this problem swiftly and efficiently.

Try this

Test out this strategy with the two ends of your ability spectrum in one class. What differences do you immediately notice when working with the students in this way? What ways to do you differentiate the feedback between the two abilities?

Encourage doubt

"How do we know they are telling the truth?"
"Can they prove it?"
"I don't believe you!"

As a father and teacher, I positively encourage a level of healthy cynicism. This isn't to make the children doubt everything with enforced suspicion, more to challenge facts and opinions which both expand their world and help them further explore the provenance of their ideas. By encouraging doubt, you are forcing children to question facts and opinions as a 'given,' you are implicitly asking them to explore a range of options rather than just the one presented to them, and by widening their scope of influence, you are asking them to think more deeply about this viewpoint.

It is *never* too young to begin this, and asking leading questions, which take the students back to a level ascertaining whether they are being presented with the truth or not is a key skill in the classroom.

In teaching Maths, I always try where possible to relate any topic being taught to *"How could someone in Reception do this?"* Using this strategy not only simplifies my instruction to a point where all the stages of progress are both explained and visible, it also leads to a healthy level of interaction with our actual Reception classes, who have been sent challenges by Year Four, demonstrating that with enough stages built in, four year olds can solve long multiplication problems (genuinely!).

That isn't to say that they could solve the problems independently, or that I'd want them to; we save that for Year 1. This is not to encourage 'recipe maths,' but to give a prop to the stages which they have worked through together; it is effectively scaffolding.

The Japanese teaching technique of *Bansho* is excellent for simplifying the stages of learning, particularly for a key skill. The teacher uses a long whiteboard and demonstrates these stage from left to right at the top of the board, with student examples underneath. This allows any student who is stuck to refer to the board, identify which stage they are having difficulty with, and see what they need to do next to progress.

(Stupid Dad Awards: My five year old daughter recently asked me what 'rot' meant. "It means decomposing'" I replied...)

Try this

Examine your next topic - how could you simplify it so that a four-year-old could understand? What steps would you need to scaffold to get to the level of understanding you are seeking?

Build interest

Every four year old wants to talk and share their world with anyone who will listen - it is very often very much a one way street with conversation, and yet this tempers as they get older. Why is this? How can we address it?

By asking open questions which allow the children to expand the sharing of their world, we encourage them to more consciously think about their responses, grow their confidence and demonstrate a genuine interest in their lives.

The key question when greeted with some strange lines and what could be a circle as their artwork is not *"What is it?"* (translation: *"I have no idea what it is you've just painted"*) but rather *"tell me about this"* (aka *" That's interesting, I bet there's lots going on in this picture"*).

re-framing a closed question to an open question that a four year old could respond to, opens doors in ways few other questions are able to manage. It isn't dumbing down, it is repackaging.

Try this

It is easy to offer complacent interest in a student's work; they however can detect insincerity from an early age. Take a skill from Early Years - go to their level (if possible), make eye contact, and let their work/item/object form a triangle between the two of you. Ask questions only they can answer, and smile.

Open questions

Open questions are ones where there is no definite one word answer being sought. In examination terms, these are questions which begin with *discuss*, *debate* or *contrast*. These are ambitious questions to ask, especially aloud, since they require a structure to build against which can be incredibly challenging (even as adults).

Open questions have the same danger as Fat Questions, as they might lead you in a direction you hadn't planned for, and they can have the danger of being something of an indulgence which costs learning time for the rest of the class. This is as opposed to fat questions, where a topic or theme is being explored more informally. To that end, and this sounds counter-intuitive, try to give a boundary for open questions; think of them as semi-open! This may be either with a time or word limit, or a numerical limit on examples. For example:

"Can anyone think why we might need to have units of time?"

Could be more effectively explored by adapting as below:

"Can we think of three reasons we need to have units of time?"

or

"Can you tell everyone in under ten words why it's important to have units of time?"

Some teachers employ open questions very effectively to operate as summaries of a lesson or learning intention. If this is the case, there is even more need to define a clear boundary. Could students answer them on a Post-it for example, or in a Twitter mock-up, restricting the answer to 140 characters?

To ensure learning time is protected with open questions, set out your intended goals for the questions. Is it to have students verbally model for their peers, or correcting/improving or adding to one another's answers? Clarifying this in your head beforehand will make you less likely to go off-point in your teaching time.

Try this:

Open questions are good for encouraging higher level thinking, therefore promoting progress, rather than simple regurgitation. Be wary of using them as filler, which they can do with ease. Instead plan them carefully, insuring they have a purpose. Decide your end goal for the pupils - what you want them to progress in or achieve by answering a fat question - and work back from that point.

Questions to Assess

One of the vital purposes of questions in a classroom is to assess. They can be used assess the students prior knowledge of a topic before beginning, assess the students knowledge of the ideas you've just imparted on them, or assess the depth of their understanding. Most importantly this information, gleaned through assessment, will form the basis of what you do next as a teacher, what steps you take in the lesson and in the planning of subsequent lessons.

Hinge questions

These questions are those which fall at a point in the lesson where a transition will take place, a hinge point. This is the point during the lesson where you move to the next key idea or concept. This moment in the lesson is vital due to the fact that the ideas and activities are intrinsically linked and build on one another. The understanding of the content or ideas prior to the hinge is a prerequisite for what follows. The answers received to a question at this point in the lesson will determine the direction the lesson will take. As such, these hinge questions must be very carefully constructed by the teacher, they must be designed with precision.

A hinge question should through its design, inform the teacher if it is appropriate to move on with the planned lesson. If we misjudge this decision then, however immaculately planned our lessons might be, the pace and progress of our students will falter. Without a hinge question which accurately identifies potential misconceptions, we run the risk of diving in to the rest of our lesson regardless and leaving our students floundering on the shore.

Conversely if we in error assume lack of understanding, our students are left listening to a pointless recap and slowly the light of engagement in each of them dims. For these reasons Dylan Wiliam talks of these decisions being the most important decisions we make, but do we make them consciously enough and do we devote the thought and planning into the construction of the questions they are based upon?

Planning Hinge questions

To plan a hinge question which is truly effective is not an easy feat. The first hurdle to overcome is ensuring your own clarity. You need to be clear of your learning intentions for the lessons and how the ideas build and develop. In addition to this, it's important to consider the possible misconceptions which may occur in the development of the ideas.

A hinge question is not one where elaborate answers are required; ideally the students should all be able to give a quick response to the question. The students should be able to give immediate responses and the teacher get a 'snapshot' of their understanding. This is not the opportunity for developing lengthy answers or following up with probing questions. In turn the teacher should be able to carry out rapid analysis of the responses received.

The manner in which the question is asked is also important here. All students need to give a response in order for the teacher to make a valid judgement. This is where the trusty white boards or voting kits come in useful. It is worth spending time explaining the purpose of these points in the lesson and stressing the need for individual responses.

Finally, and the reason constructing these questions can be devilishly tricky, the teacher needs to know why the students have given the responses they have. The question must be one to which it is impossible for the students to give the right answer through incorrect means. Which is of course easier said than done.

Questioning for assessment

In the excellent 'Teach Like a Champion' book, it outlines the power of using questions for assessment. It recommends just five, to broadly fit the range of abilities in the classroom. This is a very clever approach of using a *broad* tool to get a *broad* assessment in a very *narrow* space of time.

The fascinating aspect of this however is the way you craft your questions. It is a really interesting process to design a question which gets an accurate measure of an effective learning experience, beyond the 'give me an example of...' question. How would you craft a question which assessed the learning of the less able in a lesson about categorising minibeasts, or types of metal, or apostrophes?

The way I would suggest tackling this would be to go back to the learning intention, and drive the questions from this. The lower ability question would examine the first steps of the learning intention - how secure is their understanding? The middle three questions would ideally examine the learning intention from three different angles (so times tables could be looked at as a simple sum, a word problem or as an array for example) and the final question would be to measure how learning had progressed or connected with other knowledge *beyond* that of the original intention.

This is actually the fun part - if you were carrying this out for the first time, you could well design your lesson *back* from this point, trying to solve how you could get those answers correctly designed through your teaching. Doing this task will make you rethink the format in which you approach tasks in lessons in a new and fresh manner. Clearly, this produces a qualitative rather than quantative result, but this will feed into your future planning and teaching, which is more fundamental an approach to assessment.

Try this

Assess your next lesson using only five questions at the end. Does the result match your prediction?

Closed questions

These are also seen as 'cloze' questions, where they operate as a fill-in-the-gap for incomplete sentences. They seek one word or phrase as an answer, and are very often factually-based, testing knowledge. As teachers, these tend to be the default question type we ask, and are useful in establishing one child's recall of that fact, yet we accept them as an answer for the whole. They are excellent for the purpose of testing knowledge in a variety of topics, so that you might quickly assess the depth of knowledge retained by your students.

In order to fully harness the power of the closed question, try to engineer opportunities where you can get as many closed answers in one question as possible. The power of a mini whiteboard, number fan or speed survey cannot be underestimated in order to achieve this. While the first two of these should be familiar to most teachers, a speed survey is a rapid-recall of answers from a range of children. This is done in two ways; either by asking the same question to several children, or asking for confirmation of children's opinions to an answer.

Same question - *"Can four people name a type of triangle?"*

Confirmation - *"Sam thinks it is a right-angled triangle. Can you make potato fists if you agree?"*

Hands Up: Questions to ignite thinking in the classroom

Classroom Organisation

Questions can do a whole lot more than simply finding answers - careful questioning can be used to improve levels of behaviour, streamline classroom admin and save large amounts of time.

The best questions can also help support a needy classroom. This section touches on some of these key areas.

Who?

This can be used in two ways; as a classroom filter (*"who can tell me where we might find the capital of Spain?"*) or as a way of identifying a character or person in a topic (*"who caused the break with Rome?"*)

The classroom filter provides extraneous information which slows down filter time. The way you can tell if someone has the answer is if they indicate this themselves, so why would you add this prefix? Simply asking *"Where might we find the capital of Spain?"* is more direct, and also emphasises the key aspect of the question; Where - a location.

As a behaviour management technique, who is effective when packaged with a pre-emptive statement about expected conduct. "Who can put their hand up and tell me..." defines classroom behaviour, as well as indicating that calling out is not acceptable. Used carefully, this filter can underline positive classroom practice.

Using *who* at the start gives a clear signpost to the students that it is a person they are looking to identify. This should make life easier, as it offers them a limited range of answers.

You can use this question with characters in mind, or through recall. If the students are recalling someone, and can't answer your question, it may be that they don't have enough initial information to access recalled information. Prefix this by giving a context for example, *"We spoke last week about Tudor Royalty and their influence on religion."*

Try this

*Listen out for how you use **who** - is it to gain an audience or to direct students to an answer? How could you prevent this?*

Cancel out the questions

"How do we fill in the sheet?"
"What do we do next?"
"What part of the sheet do we fill in first?"

It is always important to check the understanding of instructions, either implicitly or explicitly. Any pupil who does know what they are supposed to do to proceed (and thus progress) is losing precious learning minutes. Therefore, giving clear instruction is a valuable aspect of learning admin, but as with everything, it is not guaranteed every time.

The Rule of Three occurs when the same essential question gets asked. If in a class, three students ask essentially the same question, assume that there are at least another three who are thinking the same but haven't asked, and yet another three who are doing something the wrong way. This normally equates to a third of the class off-task, and is ripe for a lesson pause and reclarification of the task.

As teachers, we can often be reactive in the way that we might say, "*how many times do I have to explain this*," but if the class don't understand, you have a failed activity, leading to a failed objective.

In this situation, it is best to stop, and retrace your steps, starting with the small wins, and underlining what needs to occur, with reassuring *"does that make sense?"* statements.

   This may seem hugely obvious to the point of trivia, but in observed lessons, and my own practice, the time taken to re-explain a directionless task would with hindsight be better spent re-explaining what needs to happen to everyone. Too often, it is seen as a failure to stop and reiterate, when re-establishing your goals for the task or lesson are a much more beneficial use of time.

This again is where the *Bansho* or stepped approach works well, especially visually. It is the educational equivalent of the multitude of props used on children's art programmes, with each item showing the progress of the item.

One technique which may seem very curious but when employed well works wonders is to walk through each stage. Imagining a line across your teaching space, working from right to left, you step into each section. Do this twice, then repeat a third time, but asking the students to explain that particular stage. A *walking explanation* can visually cut through any questions, as it front-loads any difficulties.

Try this

Trial the walking explanation in a lesson involving a procedural task, using defined steps and stages.

Skinny questions

"How much is that in pence?"
"What is the population in Madrid?"
"Where would you put an apostrophe?"

These are one word or phrase answers which cut out the context and demand recall. Excellent for helping to filter through other data, thin questions are often used in terms of comprehension, knowledge testing and factual replies. They are the equivalent of a Google search or a pub quiz.

What they don't do is explain the origin of the answer, so there is a danger with a skinny answer that it is either right or wrong. I suggest that this is a danger because this may not be your intention! The first example above is being used to test whether a child can convert an amount of money - in this case a right/wrong answer is needed to see whether they are able to do this!

The third question however could be testing any number of things - recall, comprehension, even simple research. Ensure you know your intention when asking a thin question, or just whether an answer is right or wrong.

It can be very useful to have students write their own skinny questions after reading a passage for prose. This checks for understanding, and can be used for pair and share assessment strategies too.

While skinny questions aren't particularly useful for checking deeper understanding or for promoting progress, they are essential for clarity when checking instructions about behaviour or when student organisation is ambiguous. They are particularly perfect for mini-plenaries - an ideal time to use mini-whiteboards too.

Try this

Skinny questions trim any fat from an answer, so work exceptionally well in knowledge-based inquiry. Only use these at the beginning of a lesson if you need to establish previous knowledge, rather than wanting to establish the depth of understanding your students may have.

The power of preparation

In 'Teach like a Champion,' Doug Lemov advocates teachers crafting their questions to the students with care and precision beforehand. This appears to be in contrast to the current thought process of planning which seems to suggest that time and experience offer a justification to reduce written planning, as the Five Minute Plan indicates (although it still asks you to consider key aspects of the lesson) Certainly, this makes sense, since the plan for a lesson should be for you and ideally no-one else. It should be the key details to help prompt you in achieving your aims.

So why craft your questions? By spending real conscious thought on these beforehand, you are completely guided by the lesson objective, and not by anything which may happen in the lesson. Yes, this takes no account of tangents, but does force you to address your objectives purely and without influence.

The easiest way to begin to do this is to rephrase your objectives as a question, and build back from that. As an example, consider the following:

Objective: *Recognise the main types of angle in a triangle*

Turning this into the main question for the lesson, you now have a framework for building toward that final question.

Main: *Can you identify all the angles in these three questions?*

Subsidiary:
What is an angle?
What is a triangle?
What are angles measured in?
Why are some angles in triangles different to others?
What is the difference between an acute and obtuse angle?
...

I have found that when I plan back using questions, my lesson, and the tasks, become more clear and apparent to me far more easily than if I base it on the objective alone, since it forces me to examine the answer I am hoping the children will offer, and this helps to guide what task would lead them to this answer.

Try this
Write out three questions for your next lesson. Consider key questioning moments in the lesson, and the types of question appropriate to those moments.

Questioning for behaviour management

Questioning can be a useful weapon in a teachers arsenal to help maintain student attention and behaviour. Although I'd never advocate behaviour to be the primary motivator behind a teachers questions, planned and delivered well, questioning can have the effect of promoting good behaviour.

Whole Class Expectations
Whether you are a classroom teacher in a primary, with the same 20 students in your care, day in and day out, or a secondary Drama teacher who sees your year 8 class once a fortnight, establishing expectations is key. By establishing high expectations of students early and consistently enforcing them, you ensure that your classroom is one conducive to learning at all points.

There are many ways in which to establish expectations and continually reinforce them. In reality as a professional you will employ many techniques; however teacher talk can play a big part of this. By considering carefully the phrases used during questioning you can implicitly (and at times explicitly) reinforce the expectations of behaviour.

By the same token you can undermine your own expectations through mismanagement of whole class questioning. Have you ever stopped to consider the message you are sending to the students when you allow students to shout out answers or questions? It is tempting, particularly if it is a valid question posed from the student, to answer it but by doing this we undermine ourselves.

Then there is the student whose contributions are taken repeatedly so as to avoid his energy being directed towards the more disruptive. What of the students who are multi-tasking? Is this acceptable during a class discussion?

The following techniques can be helpful to consider when conducting whole class questioning. Through regular use they will quickly become second nature;

*   Develop some stock phrases when starting questions. "Who can put their hand up and tell me...?" reminds the students how you would like them to contribute. "Without shouting out, who could explain..." is more explicit. "Who will be able to explain to the class...?" implies to the class that they will be expected to listen to their classmate. By specifying that they are explaining to the class, by default 'the class' will be required to listen to this answer.

Hands Up: Questions to ignite thinking in the classroom

- Just as you wouldn't talk over a student, don't allow them to do this either. Stop a student if during their answer others are talking. Although it may cause minor frustration to the student contributing, they will recognise that their contribution is being valued. Apologise to the student contributing and explain why you have stopped them. "I'm sorry Emily, I'm just going to ask you to pause there. You're giving an excellent answer, however not everyone in the class is listening as they should be."
- Thank those doing the correct thing. "Thank you Chris for raising your hand. How would you answer this question?"
- Allow guesses but never accept 'I don't know' and move on. There will be occasions where students genuinely don't know the answer to the questions, and those where they are attempting to avoid active participation in the lesson. Ensure there is an expectation set and reinforced that students will not be allowed to get away with no response. The following section outlines some strategies you could use to tackle this.

Managing the Needy Class

A needy class can cause a number of issues, most notably the stunted pace that come as a result of their uncertainty and their requirement to question every last instruction. These are questions which are time consuming, of questionable relevance and add nothing to the learning occurring in the classroom. They must be stopped. The first step is to recognise that your class is heading this way before you find yourself being questioned by a group of 12 year olds about exactly what shade of blue they should use to colour their Bunsen Burner.

The beast that is a needy class, is entirely one of the teachers making. It tends to be borne as a result of the teacher answering all of the questions fired at him or her at the start of a task. Understandably, once setting a task, the teacher wishes to get started and so in the interest of time saving will answer all of the students questions. Unchecked, over time these questions grow, not in quality but in quantity.

The same question is asked numerous times and individuals seem to require reassurance over every detail of the task. The first thing when going into battle against this beast is to check that you are absolutely clear in your instructions (PRIME is useful to check , see earlier...?). In the worst cases, a needy class may even interrupt mid-way through instructions, to ask abut the instructions.

Here non-verbal signals for them to lower their hands should be deployed. A finger calmly placed to your lips to signal quiet or a pat of the air to indicate they should put their hands down are useful to avoid having to give these instructions verbally.

Next, whatever happens, do not ask, "does anyone have any questions?" Instead, ask a student to explain the instructions again; you may wish to ask two or three students to do this one after the other. After this, you can ask them the questions. Clarify the details by interrogating your volunteers. If a question is asked of you, repeat it back to the class and ask a student to answer. In this instance avoid repeating the students answer. Remember, you are trying to end their reliance on you, and instead force them to listen to each other.

Another technique can be to, following instructions, only allow the students to ask a maximum of five questions about the task as a collective. They need to consider very carefully the questions they are going to ask and ensure that it counts. Its amazing how quickly the student who asks if it is acceptable to use a pencil for their diagram, has their question answered by their peers in an attempt to avoid losing one of their questions.

Don't be lulled into a false sense of security however, there is one last battleground you must tackle before you can claim to have defeated the 'needy class'. The students have begun the task, there is a quiet calm which lasts for mere seconds and then hands begin to raise, first one or two, then more. A whine of 'sir...?' comes from the corner then again another and another.

The questions you thought you had pre-empted have not been squashed but transferred from the public forum to an individual basis. If you are not prepared for this you can quickly find yourself paying a bizarre version of the 'Whack-a-mole' fun fair game.

Firstly, it is important to remove the expectation that you will rush to their aid. You have already ensured that the students are clear about the logistics of the task, they know what they should be doing and how. They also know what resources are available to them and what they should be drawing upon to help them complete the task. As a result the only valid questions they should have must be linked to the knowledge required to complete the task.

If the task has been designed to be accessible to all or has appropriate differentiation then it is highly unlikely that these immediate questions are valid ones; the students are simply seeking reassurance.

For tasks the students are completing individually, remain at the front of the classroom and as the hands creep upwards wave them back down, tell the students "no questions for the next three minutes". You will want to wander the class, a voice inside will be telling you to circulate but stick to your guns. Remain at your post, you will need to be vigilant. Only when your designated time is up should you venture tentatively into the foray. The idea is that by this point the students will be engrossed in their task and hopefully will have let go of their initial, superficial questions. This will leave you free to deal with those questions which matter.

Another tactic is the classic, see three before me (Bill Rogers ?) and I've known a number of teachers who will have displayed prominently in their classrooms 'C3B4ME' for easy reference. This is a very useful reminder for the students to utilise their peers as a source of information, although you should never let it become a cocktail party of chat, with students wandering around aimlessly.

There will always be classes who for one reason or another do not trust the information they receive from their peers and want to rely on you as the 'expert'. Asking the students to indicate the urgency of their question using traffic light cards will help you prioritise. Train the students to have these out on their desks as a matter of course. If they are working without issue the green card is on display, if they have a question but can continue with the task they display the orange card and if they have a question which they require answering before the can continue they display the red card. This technique has the effect of forcing the students to evaluate the urgency of their question but also helps you as a teacher to prioritise. In the event you look across the classroom and see a sea of red cards, it is likely time to stop the task and identify the issue.

Questioning Questioning

The following article first appeared in the January 2015 edition of UKEdchat Magazine.

Have you noticed how, just after you book a holiday, you see information about that location everywhere? It's like it has suddenly appeared on your radar. The same could be said for answering your own questions.

It wasn't until I read a statistic that suggested teachers answered up to 80% of their own questions that I became actively aware of how much I was guilty of this too. and so my journey into exploring questions in the classroom began.

Questions are, I believe, a key factor in the success or otherwise of a classroom. Asking the best questions can encourage children to be inquisitive, think more deeply, progress further; even improve their own questioning skills themselves.

Bad questions operate merely to confirm something a teacher assumes, and doesn't embed learning in a way a good question can, and does. Here are my top five tips for questioning in the classroom.

Avoid question widows

These are questions either without a purpose or an audience. Challenge yourself - before you ask a question in class, ask yourself, 'what is the purpose of this question?' - is it to test the children on something you've taught them? Is it to hear what you want to hear, or is it to offer a small incremental step toward greater understanding? If a three year old shows you a messy smudge of paints, is it better to ask 'what is it?' or 'tell me about this.'?

Decide if you want open or closed answers

Closed answers seek simple answers generally speaking. Open questions challenge assumptions, and force students to justify their stance. The best closed questions are quickfire and recap, and the best way to force open questions to be deeper is to be tenacious and keep asking 'Why?' - act like a four year old!

Never say the same question twice

If they can't understand the question the first time around, they probably won't the fifth time either. I call this reframing. Use the key words again, but reframe the question, directing the students toward the sort of answer you are seeking.

Use names carefully, if at all

If you say a student's name before asking a question, you are mentally letting everyone else off the hook. I use potato fists in this situation - everyone else puts one potato out if they think they have the answer, two if they are definite. Saying a student's name at the end however is sometimes used to admonish someone who isn't concentrating - not the purpose! Try not using names, and instead 'look' for someone to answer. Hands up or down doesn't matter - thinking about the right answer does.

Audit your questioning skills

This takes confidence! Have a colleague sit in one of your lessons and note down on your table plan the people you ask questions to, and have them note down open and closed questions, and how many times you allow others to answer your questions (and the ones you answer yourself). Look carefully at what you find out - and change your practice!

Killer Questions

This is a bonus chapter from guest writer, Toby French, who also writes on the www.staffrm.io teacher network.

Here's a question I ask about my lessons all the time: is what students most enjoy about my subject the same as what they need to learn? It seems to me that enjoyment is a happy by-product of great learning. If students are talking about a lesson in the playground – Sir, are we playing that spying game like the other class? – we feel successful, but what I want to create is a longer-term curiosity that might lead to great learning over time: Sir, how are we going to find out the answer?

Students in history classrooms across the world love to hear the most gruesome details. However, unless they're studying torture through time the most disgusting information is often superfluous. Whilst we want students to satisfy their own queries, we also need to steer the conversation along a more mature path. And therein lies the problem: I now find C18 crop-yields really interesting, but I also remember being twelve and liking castles. So, what questions can we help students ask in order to keep the curiosity moving with an end-goal in sight?

This image of a Berkshire sow opened the study of agricultural revolution in Britain. I stuck a target on it and asked Y8 to come up with their Killer Question: out of all of the great questions they could think of what would really kick the topic off? To help formulate the questions I used a shamelessly pilfered deeper questioning grid to push for more thoughtful lines of enquiry.

Hands Up: Questions to ignite thinking in the classroom

The question Y8 eventually came up with, after exhausting and tweaking many possibilities, was 'Why is that pig so fat?' And you know what? That's the question I wanted to answer as well. I even had it written on the next slide. As such they were able to have ownership over the core question for half a term. At the end of each hour I asked: So, are we any closer to finding out why that pig is so fat? What sort of information do we need? Where are we going to find this? Who could we ask? Could we write an essay on this yet? Are there any recurring themes so far? Is any of our evidence unnecessary? I could easily have spent a whole term answering this question, with each mini-topic offering more advanced and in-depth history.

But what's really great about a killer question is that the subject has driven the conversation. The teacher has presented it, yes; but the students have taken ownership. They're much more likely to investigate those crop yields thoroughly if they're trying to solve a mystery that they've framed.

In his excellent TED Talk on high school maths, Dan Meyer strips a classic textbook question, bloated with exam-speak, to its most basic problem. He shows a video of a large water tank filling up until one fed-up student asks: Sir, how long is it going to take for this thing to fill up? Here the maths has driven the conversation. In my example it was the history.

The key for a really killer question is the stimulus: beads representing the atomic structure of water at the door to the science lab; the chalk outline of a body on the floor of the history class; some kind of ash substitute on the geography tables; a giant shell, placed throne-like, in the middle of the English room; having to wear the kippah on entry to RE; taking shoes off anywhere. All these lead to fantastic questions if we can help the students formulate them. Eventually students begin to ask their own great questions, smashing two or three together. Perhaps some, with a bit of prompting, will say, Given that we looked at x last lesson, is it possible that ..? They might even create their own hypotheses using the stimulus, their understanding of killer questions and their contextual knowledge. And when this does happen I want to leap about with joy!

What I like about the killer question is that with a bit of steering it becomes the hook on which to hang the more academic learning. It creates that long-term curiosity which might just lead to great learning over time.

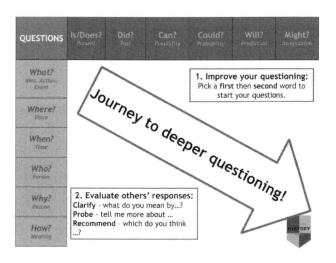

https://www.youtube.com/watch?v=NWUFjb8w9Ps&feature=youtu.be

Well? What did you think?

The most important question about this book is 'was it helpful for you?' We at *Teacherly* want to reward your efforts to feedback to us, so have developed a reward system for your next order through us. Each of these efforts earns at least 10% off your next order:

10% off - if you write a 3+ review on Amazon
10% off - if you write a blogpost review
10% off - if you include a link to Teacherly
10% off - if you reference this book in a public talk
10% off - if you have a review in printed form

Just send us a screenshot or other to <u>hello@teacherly.cc</u> and we'll send your voucher back. We'll also send you an exclusive ebook - 'Ten Dynamite Questions for meetings' as a thank you!

If you can think of any other way to share this book, please do let us know, and we'll organise a reward as thanks to you.

The Teacherly Team

Smallprint: Maximum order size - £100. Discount not available 30 days after purchase.

16926605R00095

Printed in Great Britain
by Amazon